"Astonishing in its directness and simplicity, this memoir of the Holocaust and Communist Poland delivers a gripping account of one man's terrifying journey from orphan child to war refugee to American citizenship."

—**Leonard Kniffel**, Past President of Polish American Librarians Association & Author of *A Polish Son in the Motherland: An American's Journey Home*

"A personal account of political upheavals, moral dilemmas and perseverance, Haska & Naumann's book is written with passion and an intense attention to detail chronicling the lethal conditions of Nazi and Soviet occupations of Poland as well as the blessings of living the American dream. It is a story of integrity, prudence, sound judgement and sagacity, revolving around a compelling thought that 'education is the only thing that could never be taken away from us.'"

—**Dr. Arthur R. Rachwald**, Professor Emeritus, U.S. Naval Academy, Visiting Professor, Diplomatic Academy of Vienna

"Stefanie Naumann brings her grandfather's compelling story to life with clarity and compassion. This well-written, immensely readable chronicle flows like a novel, exhibiting the vulnerabilities, strengths and ultimately the courage of its characters. Dr. Naumann's work speaks to the inherent and eternal dignity of the human spirit, something in which every reader can rejoice."

—**Greg Fields**, Author of *Arc of the Comet*, 2018 Kindle Book of the Year Nominee

"An engaging true story of how life survival depended on language mastery. The ability to adapt and willingness to learn new languages proved to be lifesaving to Tadeusz Haska on many occasions. After mastering languages, Tadeusz then turned it into his career. Great read!"

—**Gregory Kojak**, Chairman, The Polish American Association

"Those of us who are children, grandchildren, and great-grandchildren of immigrants need to remember and keep the legacies of their struggles alive. As in the case of Tadeusz and Jadwiga Haska, my grandparents fled conflict in Europe and eventually came to the United States through Ellis Island to raise families and become the very fabric and steel that makes our democracy great. Enjoy this historical read!"

—**Steve Loeffler**, Rear Admiral, U.S. Navy (Retired)

"Stefanie Naumann has done an admirable job of honoring her grandfather's memory, survival, and accomplishments. As fewer and fewer survivors of World War II remain, these first-person accounts are critical testimony and witness of what it takes to survive during war and in the face of great adversity. This story should resonate with other Polish Americans and their descendants. It also offers encouragement to other immigrants that yes, with drive, a quick wit, and a healthy dose of luck, it is possible to achieve the seemingly impossible goal of rebuilding a new life."

—**Katrina Shawver**, Author of *HENRY: A Polish Swimmer's True Story of Friendship from Auschwitz to America*

"A deeply moving personal account of the resilience of the human spirit in the face of war, its aftermath, and the dislocations it causes. It will be grimly familiar to many whose families have experienced the same, and an eye-opener for the fortunate ones who haven't."

—**Ted Mirecki**, President, DC Division of the Polish American Congress; writer, translator

"Haska's story embodies the principal theme of survival during war —the ordinary individual finding the strength and courage to endure, perhaps even to save his loved ones. Living in a time of peace and blessed with the abundance of America we need to retell this story. Tadeusz's memoir is unique in that he maintained his freedom and survived by tapping his talent for languages. This paid additional dividends after the war, allowing him to prosper in the United States."

—**Peter Obst**, Poles in America Foundation

"Stefanie Naumann's book is a fascinating story about the author's grandfather, who managed to escape jail in Stalinist Poland, and eventually settled in the United States of America, where he became a professor. Poland lost an extremely talented man."

—**Jan Sroka**, Historian of Pomerania, Dziedzictwo Foundation, Sławno, Poland

How Languages Saved Me:
A Polish Story of Survival

by Tadeusz Haska and
Stefanie Naumann

© Copyright 2019 Tadeusz Haska and
Stefanie Naumann

ISBN 978-1-63393-923-3

StefanieNaumann.com

Published by

 köehlerbooks™

210 60th Street
Virginia Beach, VA 23451
800–435–4811
www.koehlerbooks.com

HOW LANGUAGES SAVED ME

A POLISH STORY OF SURVIVAL

Tadeusz Haska
and Stefanie Naumann

VIRGINIA BEACH
CAPE CHARLES

DEDICATION

To my husband, David Naumann, and children, Emily and Alex Naumann, for your love and support.

And in loving memory of Tadeusz, Jadwiga, and Christine Haska, the most important role models in my life.

—Stefanie Naumann

PREFACE

My grandfather, Tadeusz Haska, was born in 1919 in Mikołajki, Poland. He was one of two siblings of six to survive childhood. He and his brother Antoni lived alone after losing both parents by the age of thirteen. Tadeusz used his knowledge of nine languages to survive World War II by translating German newspapers to farmers and job instructions to French prisoners of war and impersonating a German on occasion. After the war, Tad escaped jail by the Soviet Secret Police, fled to Sweden and eventually reunited with his wife, Jadwiga, by smuggling her in a coffin on a ship. This book is Tad's extraordinary account of how his knowledge of languages helped him survive before, during, and after World War II.

After immigrating to the U.S., Tadeusz earned his Ph.D. at the University of California, Berkeley in Linguistics in his ninth language—English. He taught, and served as chairman, in the Polish Department at the Defense Language Institute for thirty-five years. My grandfather was a great and relentless teacher. He never gave up on people, and he made them see their own promise even when they insisted they were incapable of learning. Many of his students continued to visit and correspond with him long after graduation and their own retirements.

He was dedicated to the mission of the Defense Language Institute Foreign Language Center and believed that its impact was instrumental for our nation's security. He was an eternal student of history, culture, and language. Many conversations ended with him documenting his evidence that there were two centers of the universe—the United States and Poland! Because of that, we tucked a bit of Polish soil in his pocket after he passed away.

In addition to his career accomplishments, he was one of the kindest, most patient, and most tolerant men in the world. His gentle kindness and generous spirit touched everyone he knew. His family served as the center of his life. He and Jadwiga celebrated their 50th anniversary with a private audience with Saint John Paul II in Rome surrounded by their family.

I got to hear many of his life stories growing up that provided invaluable reference points about what is truly important and right. My grandparents faced unspeakable adversity, and they taught me what the courage of conviction means. They came to the United States because my grandfather fiercely believed in independence and the voice of the people being heard in government. My grandmother just wanted to get far away from the people who would have rather imprisoned my grandfather.

Everyone who knew my grandfather knew that he was dignified and kind. Until about the time he was eighty, he still put on a jacket to answer the front door. He would greet an older lady friend by kissing her hand. He always had time to listen to people's stories—even when there didn't seem to be time for him to tell his own. He set an example of integrity and faith that benefitted everyone around him.

He made a difference in this world in several ways. First, he was a wonderful family patriarch. He never raised his voice to any of us, and he always had time for us. He never told us what to do, but when he could not get people to see what they should do themselves, he did take a more direct approach. A couple of decades ago, we were having Christmas Eve dinner in the Polish tradition, which includes the opłatek—the communion host. The patriarch of the family breaks off a piece and gives it to each family member present with a wish for the future. Usually, it's health and happiness or something like that. But this one year, my grandfather broke off a piece and gave it to my husband, David. He said, "You have been married for six years. I wish for you to have a baby before I am dead!" We all just about fell off our chairs. David stammered and said "Yes, yes, Dziadzia (Grandpa in English)—we will have a baby right away!" And we did—Emily came the following year, and our son Alex a few years later. Both children were born on my birthday, through no sort of planning, but happy surprises. They were my grandfather's pride and joy.

He also made a difference because he never held a grudge. He said that the single most wonderful thing about America is that you always got a second chance. In so many countries—to whom you are born, whether you grew up in a city or farm, or the bank account of your parents indelibly marked your future. Not so in America. And he embodied that spirit by never holding a grudge against anyone and always giving second chances.

He did not tolerate intolerance or prejudice or hatred. When I was a young girl and asked him the meaning of some epithet, he told me that it was unimportant what it meant in the literal sense— that it was more important to know that those words were part of a language of ignorant people. He went on to explain that nations always begin calling people in opposing nations demeaning names as a first step in dehumanizing them and making them easier to oppress. He would have none of it.

If I had to pick the one thing my grandfather was passionate about—it was life itself. Because of what he saw and experienced in Poland during the war and Nazi occupation, he was fiercely protective of human life. He was opposed to any jeopardy of human life, and he was passionate about the celebration of the human spirit wherever he saw it. And, he saw the best of that spirit in his family first and foremost.

My grandfather wore a large, heavy wedding band—the band that my grandmother's mother brought from Poland when she came to live with them in 1955. It was a blended ring from her father's wedding band and her husband's. She took my grandfather's wedding band to a jeweler and had that gold blended with the one she brought from Poland. That ring represents my grandfather's passion for life and his honoring of the lives blended into it.

The last thing I would like you to know about my grandfather is that I was the apple of his eye. I felt like the luckiest girl in the world to be his only granddaughter. Every summer when I was a child, I would visit him and my grandmother *(Dziadzia* and *Babcia*, in Polish) and they would rearrange their lives around my visit. Every morning they would ask me what I wanted to do that day, and that's what we would do. They gave me the gift of time—playing games, going for a picnic, to the Viennese bakery, Dennis the Menace Park, Thrifty drugstore to get fifteen-cent ice cream, walks in the forest or the beach. We would go on such long walks that my mom would worry something had happened to us. I am so grateful to have all these wonderful memories to carry with me for the rest of my life. He always made me feel like I was the most important thing to him. He never asked for my hugs first, but my first hugs were always for him. He never pushed me academically, but he applauded the loudest. He was the first generation in our family to earn a Ph.D., and, because of him, I was the third.

After Poland was liberated this last time, my grandfather, mother, and I went to Poland with my grandfather as the tour guide. It was a sentimental journey in so many ways, and I'll never forget his rosy cheeks and the sparkle in his blue eyes when he spoke to me in Polish, giving me the history of a particular place or artifact. Every week we would talk on the phone, and he would help me practice my Polish. My grandpa also infused our family's connection with his beloved Poland in my own children. After his death, my daughter went to sleep with her Polish dolls and a Polish wreath on her head—just to feel close to her Dziadzia. A few weeks later, my son reminded us that we needed to continue the Polish tradition of going outside with his father on Christmas Eve to look for the first star, signaling that it is time to open the first Christmas gift.

Tadeusz started writing his memoir in the early 1990s but had not finished it at the time of his passing in 2012 at age ninety-three. I had two motivations in publishing this book. First, I believe that preserving eyewitness accounts is critical to learning about World War II and its effects on civilians. Each year there are fewer individuals alive who have firsthand knowledge of those effects. Second, after the death of my dear mother, Christine Haska, in 2017, my last direct connection with Poland, I became even more determined to honor my Polish heritage.

While cleaning out my mother's garage, I found numerous audio and video recordings of my grandfather being interviewed about his life. I used these recordings, as well as his journals and the letters he wrote to my grandmother, to complete his memoir in his own words. Birgitta Bergstrom, the daughter of the Swedish family who helped my grandparents after they escaped Poland as political refugees, provided me with even more audio recordings of her interviews of my grandparents about their lives when she visited them in the 1990s. Izolda Blicharska-Odrzykoska, the daughter of my grandfather's high school girlfriend in Poland, helped by confirming some details of his earlier years. I was fortunate to have the help of Polish cousins Magda Kopec, Andy Bartkowski, and Wanda Białkowska, and a genealogist in Poland, Piotr Haska, who shares the last name of my grandparents, to assist in translating my grandfather's handwriting from the backs of old photographs. Jan Sroka in Poland kindly provided me with a copy of the diary of Amelia Łaczyńska, a colleague of my grandfather's before his arrest by the Soviet Secret Police. I also am appreciative of the translation work of Ewa Hayward, the video recording work of Charlie Davis, the audio recording work of Kelsey Barton, and the video and audio transfer work of Arno Featherstone. The memoir that follows is in my grandfather's voice, as he wrote in his journal, and as I heard in his recorded interviews and his letters to my grandmother. He was a treasure to all who knew him, and his legacy will live on forever and serve as a cherished touchstone of one man's life and the difference it made.

—Stefanie Naumann
StefanieNaumann.com

TABLE OF CONTENTS

CHAPTER 1

The Early Years

Nobody believes me, but I can remember being about six months old when there was a family gathering of some kind at our home, and I was set on a buffet. I looked down on the floor and felt terrified. People were looking at me, staring, laughing, and talking. Someone took me down, probably my mother because I felt secure, and that is all I can remember.

I always wanted to write about my life experiences, but I never had enough time. Now that I have time, I think it is better to live, but my daughter Christine and granddaughter Stefanie won't let me just live. They have insisted very strongly that it is time to tell about my life's adventures. What is more, my wife Jadwiga told me bluntly that she hated people that do not keep their promises. The most important women in my life pressured me, so there is no way out this time. I must do it.

My father, Antoni, met my mother, Augusta, at a specialized trade school for dairy that they graduated from in Holland. They learned how to produce butter and cheese from milk. My parents very often spoke of cheeses with foreign-sounding names like Limburger and Swiss. My father was drafted into the German army around 1912. Poland did not exist as a country at that time. After my parents' wedding, they opened a dairy in the small village of Kurzętnik. Neighbor farmers would deliver them milk, and then my parents would make butter and wonderful cheeses from the milk to sell. My father was a master of all kinds of cheeses—Swiss, Dutch, etc. He would keep them in the cellar, a cool place without refrigeration. There were huge round fat cheeses and special boxes where he would fill an entire railroad car of cheese and send it to Warsaw, Gdansk or Berlin. He made a very good living. In addition to their business, my parents were very interested in education. They always stressed to us that we could become somebody in life only through education.

Tadeusz Haska's father, Antoni Haska, wearing the uniform of his dairy farm business about 1912 in Poland.

Just as my parents' dairy business was becoming successful, my father was called back to military service on August 1, 1914, when World War I started. My mother managed the dairy while he was away. My father didn't agree with what he was being asked to do when he was drafted by the German army because he was loyal to Poland, even though it did not officially exist. He said he was a Pole wearing a German uniform being asked to kill Russians who were often Poles wearing Russian uniforms. My father reasoned that he couldn't shoot another Pole because they were his brothers. I asked my father how many people he killed in the war. He answered, "None," because he would deliberately aim at the wrong place. He told me, "I was always praying to God that He should forgive me for pointing the gun at Him." He said he always felt bad for shooting at the window of the Lord. My father used to talk a lot about how one day people would come to their senses, be able to talk out their differences, and there would be no more war.

My father did not return until 1918, after being taken prisoner by the Russians in the very first battle at Tannenberg in East Prussia in August 1914. He had been gone so long that my mother thought he had been killed. Russians sent all prisoners into the depths of Russia. My father was sent from one camp to another until he found himself in Siberia before being sent home. November 11, 1918, was armistice day and World War I was over.

On June 28, 1919, the Treaty of Versailles was signed and formally ended the war. I was born two days later in Mikołajki, with the name Tadeusz, to commemorate the rebirth of Poland six months before my birth. It was not only the day World War I ended but the day that Poland regained independence, thanks to U.S. President Wilson, who, in his Fourteen Points, demanded the creation of a free and independent Poland with free access to the sea. In the 18th century during the American Revolutionary War, General Tadeusz Kosciuszko helped Washington gain independence in the Battle of Saratoga. Thus, I was given the name Tadeusz—this name of both a Polish and American hero was popular in Poland in the first years of independence. Generally, during that period in Poland, the first son was named after his father, but my parents were extremely patriotic and gave me the name Tadeusz, as did countless other Polish families that year. Among my Polish friends I met in Monterey thirty years later, seven people shared my name.

(Clockwise from top left:) Antoni, Augustina, Tadeusz, and Antoni Haska in Mikołajki, Poland about 1921.

A year after my birth, my brother Antoni, named after my father, was born in 1920. My sister Agnieszka was next. Unfortunately, she died of some childhood disease. Then came another brother, Alvin. Again, he died. Then another sister, Jadwiga, then a brother Jozef. They all died, except for Antoni and me. There were so many childhood diseases at the time. I don't remember how old they were when they died, but they were still babies in diapers. My parents were very sad. My brother Antoni and I were also deeply saddened by the early deaths of my brothers and sisters. We had helped take care of the younger kids.

After selling their first dairy in the village of Kurzętnik, my parents opened a new one when they moved to the village of Mikołajki. To the north is Skalan Lake. My brother and I used to sneak out on excursions to the lake and with other neighbor boys of our age. We would go down to the lake and tie some logs together to make rafts, but they would end up falling apart. Throughout the winter the lake was frozen, and we could walk one kilometer across it. But in March and April, the ice started to melt. It melted first in the middle. Along the shoreline, there was still thick ice, but it was brittle. This was the part we enjoyed. We chopped the ice and jumped from one floe of ice to another. We would dare each other to jump to another block of ice. This sounds like a foolish idea now, but this was great fun to us.

In the village center, there were three important buildings. First, there was an old church with a steeple located on slightly higher ground. Next was the village grade school across the street, which consisted of the school building, yard, and principal living quarters. Third was the village inn on the same side of the street as the school, separated by a road leading from the village's main street to some outlying farmhouses. The inn faced the village's main street. Its backyard was right on the point that extended almost throughout the entire village. My parents' house was on the upper side of the main street, in the same line of buildings with the church. It was a one-story house, as were all the village houses. It was on the higher side of the street, and there were some steps at the front entrance to the house. They ended in a level area enclosed by a wooden lattice with a roof. There were benches: one on the left and one on the right of the porch. When you opened the front door, there was the living room. There was also a kitchen and some bedrooms—at least two. One was for our family of four, and the other was occupied by my father's sister, Marianna Zakrzewska. She was a widowed seamstress and a very good one. All these quarters were in the left side of the house.

On the right side of our home was our business, the dairy. The floors in the living area were wooden boards. In the dairy, that wood had to be replaced with concrete to accommodate the government's sanitary regulations. Beneath the wooden floor was a basement for storage of cheeses. As with most of the houses in the village, our house was red brick, and the roof was covered with red tile. The square backyard had a barn made of wood. The roof was covered with tar paper and gray gravel. To the left, there was a brick building with a stable for our horse. Next to the stable was a large pigsty. The right was occupied by a wooden structure where my father kept a small horse-drawn carriage and cart for work in the field. Attached to the building was a poultry house. We had quite a few chickens, ducks, geese, pigeons, and a goat. Shortly after I was born, I almost died because I could not digest cow's milk. My mother, in desperation, asked her village midwife for advice. She told her to try goat's milk. I was saved from certain death by starvation. Since that time, there was a goat or two in our household, just in case, for medical reasons.

Behind the barn was our farmland—six acres. My father grew a patch of potatoes right behind the barn. There were also red beets, turnips, and other vegetables like cabbages and carrots. Most of the field was cultivated with rye, but there were oats and barley too. Our orchard was small—just a few apple, pear, cherry, and plum trees in front of the house. It separated the house from the village main street. Water was provided by a well on the left side of the backyard. The outhouse was hidden between the barn and poultry house.

There was no electricity in the village. Everyone used kerosene lamps. Heating the house was by burning wood or coal in tile stoves. There was a tile stove in each room. The tiles were decorative and held heat throughout the entire day and night. There were usually one or more chimneys in a house, depending on its size. I remember in the attic there was a smokehouse situated next to the chimney with an iron door. Once or twice a year before Easter or Christmas a pig was slaughtered, and the ham or sausage was smoked in the smokehouse. My father used oak tree firewood for it and called a village butcher to take care of the preparation of meats. The man did not have a butcher shop but was on call for farmers to kill pigs, to check if they were free of disease and bacteria, and to preserve the remaining meat with heavy layers of salt in between.

Our parents raised us with high expectations for good behavior without ever punishing us physically. We were instead told that if we do something stupid, we should think it over and come to our senses by ourselves. They told us that if we did not listen to them and obey them, someday they would be gone and some stranger would punish us. I have very warm recollections of my parents being affectionate toward us. My mother was quite artistic, enjoying painting, sculpting, and writing poetry. My brother is now an artist, just like our mother.

She often used folk medicine to heal our wounds. Once, I badly cut my finger with a tool that cabinet makers use. She applied to my finger a mixture of cobwebs and bread. I still have a scar to this day, but the finger eventually healed.

Both my parents were religious, but my mother was even more so. Their Catholic faith was deeply important to them, though they expressed it in different ways. My father expressed his by being a good provider. He used to say that God helps those who help themselves. My mother relied more on prayer to grow in her faith. Although I had a short time with my parents, I know that I received a good moral foundation from them.

One of the childhood stories that sticks out in my mind was a scary one for me. My uncle Paweł used to visit us for weeks at a time. When I was three years old, he took me to our pigsty at our farm and pretended he was going to put me in it. He dangled me over it for what seemed like a very long time. This terrifying experience caused me to lose my voice for six months!

I lost it until the day my brother and I were playing in the backyard where there was a tall wagon. When we climbed off the wagon, a big billy goat got loose and attacked us. My brother climbed back on, but I was too far away from the wagon and ran toward the house and up some stairs. The goat put me on his horns and threw me down. I remember screaming, "Mama!" Instead of being upset about what the goat did to me, my mother was thrilled that I had finally regained my speech after that traumatic event in the pig sty. Imagine someone who spent his life as a linguist having a six-month lapse in language ability during the formative years.

I remember that those early Christmases with my parents were very special. Christmas Eve supper involved multiple courses of non-meat dishes such as fish and vegetables. My uncle Jozef Rogatty's family would visit us because they lived only ten kilometers away. My father would make sure he came home from selling the cheeses by train in time for supper. He would bring back toys like little trains that the other kids in our village didn't even know existed. After Christmas Eve dinner, St. Nicholas would come. It was usually a neighbor dressed up, pretending to be the one who brought the toys. At first, he would ask us if we knew our prayers, and we would have to recite them. Then we would sing Christmas carols by the Christmas tree and gifts were only given to kids. On Christmas Day morning, we would find a plate under the Christmas tree with all kinds of goodies that my father brought from his business trips— candy, fresh fruit (oranges in winter were special), and some clothes. We would enjoy our new things.

I have very pleasant memories from my early childhood. It was terrible when my parents died.

My education started at the local village school on September 1, 1926, when I was seven and my brother was six. At that time, kids went to school at age seven. Since Antoni did not want to stay home, our parents asked the principal for him to be able to start school with me, even though he was six. The principal agreed. His name was Franciszek Szczepański. In 1992, when I visited Mikołajki, I had the opportunity to have a long talk with his wife Marianna, then ninety-two years old. She remembered my brother and me. She passed away in 1995. Her husband fought in the Polish Army during World War II. In 1939 he was taken prisoner by the Russians, who handed him over to the Germans, where he was sent to three prisoner-of-war camps. Thankfully, he survived the war and returned to his work as a principal.

My early school years were uneventful. When I came to school, I already knew the alphabet and how to read, because my mother had taught me these things. In my early school years, I was fascinated by church activities. My brother and I became altar boys at a young age, at least one year before we started school. One day after mass on Sunday, the pastor, Father Ludwik Chyliński, approached our family and asked us boys whether we wanted to help him at the altar. Our parents answered yes for us. Of course, we felt honored, but we were very shy. The priest was in his forties or fifties, very pleasant, but he asked if we knew Latin for the purpose of memorizing Latin responses that altar boys were expected to give during mass.

We already knew most of the responses. To us, Latin was fascinating. When the priest said things in Latin, we knew how to respond. The priest was overjoyed by our enthusiasm. We asked the sacristan and organist to teach us everything about being altar boys. We were eager learners. Since Catholic priests say mass not just on Sunday but every day, we were altar boys every day. My mother was very happy for us. Our father thought we were too young to get up so early every morning fifteen minutes before 7:00 a.m. The priest compensated us by giving us a standing invitation for breakfast after mass at his house. Breakfast was prepared by his elderly sister who was taking care of the household—usually, it was hot cocoa, a roll with butter and a slice of ham on it. On Fridays, instead of ham, there was cheese or marmalade.

Altar boys Antoni and Tadeusz Haska in Szamocin, Poland, early 1930s.

After breakfast at the priest's house, we went home and straight to school. We ran to school as if our life depended on it. Walking was for older folk like our parents. Kids were in constant motion, running. The first thing our mother did when we were altar boys was to sew surplices in the sacristy that were too large for us. She did not want us to wear oversized surplices. Our school was a large brick house with a red tile roof, consisting of one classroom where four levels of instruction took place: first through fourth grades with two teachers, one of whome was the principal and the other was the main teacher. First grade sat in the first four rows of benches arranged like a movie theater. The highest rows were occupied by fourth graders. The principal taught higher grades. I preferred the principal to the other teacher because he was less stern, more pleasant and human.

Our mother was unhappy with the quality of our school and talked with our father frequently about the time to leave Mikołajki in order to place us in another school to continue our education. She did not want us to stop our education after the fourth grade. Our father was more down-to-earth and tried to persuade her that we weren't ready financially to move. The dairy business operated with farmers who agreed with signed contracts to deliver milk daily. Otherwise, a dairy without milk could not exist. To induce farmers to sign the contract, the dairy owner had to invite farmers to his house and be on good terms to offer good prices; if not, they would go to a competitor. In other words, the dairy business was complicated because my parents had to plan a year ahead due to one-year farmer contracts. My parents discussed these long-range plans. I noticed that these discussions became more action-oriented as my parents became concerned with providing their kids with an opportunity for higher education. Eventually, they decided to sell the dairy and move to a location with better education opportunities.

1927-1928 Primary School at St. James the Apostle church in Mikołajki, Poland. Tadeusz Haska to the right of sign. Antoni Haska to the left of the sign. The principal was Franciszek Szczepański. The parish priest was Father Ludwik Chyliński.

After a severe winter in 1929, my parents sold the dairy and moved the following spring to Szamocin, a town in a different province with an elementary public school up to seventh grade. It was so far away that it was like moving from one state to another. Antoni and I quickly became altar servers at the parish church, where we learned that our priest, Bolesław Filipowski, had a colorful past. After his ordination in 1914, Father Filipowski secretly taught parish children Polish and Polish history at a time when Poland did not exist as a country. During the Wielkopolska uprising of 1918–1919, Poles launched a military insurrection against German rule. When the soldiers of Grenzschutz tried to arrest Filipowski, he managed to escape by disguising himself as a woman. He was able to get past the Germans unnoticed and joined the insurgent units, where he became their chaplain. After Poland regained its territory, Filipowski became Szamocin's parish priest, and that was about the time that Antoni and I served his church.

Because we had moved in the middle of the school year, we were placed in the same fourth grade as we were in Mikołajki. We were overwhelmed by the large size of the school. Szamocin had 1,200 people. It received city rights in 1748. With the help of a real estate agent, our parents chose this location because it is a farming town four kilometers south of a river. There were meadows extending four kilometers on the river's left bank and four kilometers on the right bank. The farmers raised cows for milk, which made it an ideal place for opening a dairy.

Back at our old home in Mikołajki, my father's dairy farm had very primitive machinery to separate fat from cheese and butter. There was no electricity in the village. He had a treadmill machine that put horses to work in a circle; their transmission of power made the separator machine work. The dairy farm produced cottage cheese, cream, and whey. From the cottage cheese, further cheeses were made. From the cream, butter was made. Whey was used for pig food and drink. When my family moved to Szamocin, electricity powered an engine with a motor for the separator, so the work was easier for my father because he did not have to pay attention to the horse.

My father had a profitable business, despite a Great Depression going on, not just in the U.S. but all over the world. By producing cheese and butter, my father could make a good profit by exporting to Germany and Warsaw. He would accompany an entire railroad wagon full of his products to sell. When he returned, it was great for my brother and me because he brought us toys such as trains, automobiles, airplanes, etc. Things were fine until, one day after dinner, my father vomited. He could not retain any food any time he ate after that. The doctor decided it was an ulcer on his stomach, and it was terminal; there was no treatment. He only lived a few months after that. Even though he was not able to eat, he wanted to be able to provide for our family, so he worked until three days before his death on July 3, 1931. I was at his bedside on that sad day when he died because my mother was doing his work delivering cheese to a railroad station.

The family suffered considerably after my father's death. Quite a few men in our village who knew the dairy business tried to marry my mother—not for love but for business purposes. But she refused to think about marrying another man. The banks started to collect from my mother, and she decided to sell everything, including the machinery of the business, and move to a nearby county seat where there was a high school. Grammar school at the time was seven years, but if anyone wanted to go to gymnasium (high school) it was necessary after fourth grade to pass an entrance exam and start with Class 1 of high school. The transition was very difficult. My mother wanted to continue the dairy business because she was trained in this area. But the farmers who delivered milk that she used to make cheese stopped when they saw a woman was in charge of the dairy business. That's why she had to sell everything. We applied for entrance to high school and passed the exam.

On September 1, 1930, we started attending high school at St. Barbara's High School in Chodzież. Everything was fine, but there was less and less money available. When my father had been alive, the farmers had delivered milk under the condition that my father would co-sign bank loans in the spring when they needed money for seed, grains, fertilizer, or other expenses. My father had agreed to this because otherwise, he wouldn't get that farmer to deliver milk to his business. But when my father died during the Depression, banks started to require the loans to be paid back. This is why my mother lost everything she owned. She had to pay back the farmers' loans they had with banks that my father had co-signed. This ruined my mother completely. She couldn't stand on her own feet. She lost everything.

Even with our family's money troubles, we persisted in attending high school. Although elementary school was free in Poland, one had to pay about 110 złoty in tuition for high school every six months.

At the time the value of the złoty was very high. Since we still lived in Szamocin and high school was in Chodzież, we traveled to school each day by train, leaving at 7:00 in the morning and returning on a 4:00 train in the afternoon. But after my father died, we no longer had enough money for the monthly railroad tickets. My brother and I were so determined that we walked fifteen kilometers to school (each way) at the age of ten and eleven years old. We woke up at 4:00 a.m. and arrived at school at 8:00 a.m. We did this from September until December, when it was very cold. For such little guys going so many miles every day was very difficult. I remember that very clearly. So, my mother looked at our misery and decided to sell everything we still had and move to Chodzież. She rented a little apartment, and we continued our first of eight years of high school.

We were quite good students, but not excellent, because of having to travel on foot before we moved and being in a completely different environment. We were somewhere in the middle between poor students and excellent students. My mother tried to find a job, but that was very, very difficult; once in a while she got some job for a few hours or days. Income was minimal, and life was very hard. Still, we were attending school, and the second year 1931–1932 went by, and we improved much more as students, but we still were not top students.

Then came 1932–1933, class 3. My father's brother came to visit us and offered us some help. Then my mother's brother came from Poznań. The year after my father died, during the summer vacation time just before the school year 1932–1933, my mother visited her brother in Warsaw. Her oldest brother, Wiktor Rogatty, lived in Poznań. Her second brother, Paweł, lived in a suburb of Warsaw and she visited him in Milanówek. When my mom died, it was summer vacation time. My brother and I were making money for the family by tutoring some rich kids while living at separate farms. We tutored kids who did not apply themselves in school. They often avoided us, and their parents had to force them to be tutored by us. The kids would frequently run away. The good part for my brother and me was that on the days that the kids didn't show up to be tutored, we got to swim and play and enjoy the summer like other kids. At the end of summer vacation in 1932, my brother and I returned to our apartment where our neighbor told us the devastating news that our mother had died while visiting her brother Paweł.

After our extended family living in other provinces learned of our mother's death, my father's brother Maksimillian came from Gdynia to see us and suggested that we move in with him. But he said he couldn't provide us with an education because he had four sons already. He was working as a railroad engineer, but his salary was low. We decided not to go with him because we wanted to continue our education. We didn't want anyone to know that our mother had passed away because my brother and I didn't want to be separated. We figured that they would send us to live in different places.

At the ages of twelve and thirteen, my brother and I started the school year 1932–1933 living alone as orphans. We decided that this was no joke; we had to study diligently. Our parents taught us that education is the only thing that could never be taken away from us. Within a year, we became top students in our classes. But we had no mother and father. We had to take care of our lives by teaching our fellow students who were so fortunate to be born into well-situated families. We tutored kids who were getting poor grades and got paid for it. We had to move to a smaller, one-room apartment that we could afford. But we survived living all by ourselves! Although we had no parents, we had the principle they instilled in us that education is the most important thing in our lives. So, we applied ourselves and, by teaching other kids, we also helped ourselves. We were models for the entire school. We could not do anything foolish. We had to always be top students. Somehow, we managed.

We tried to keep the fact that we were orphans living alone a secret, but my homeroom teacher, Professor Ivanytska, found out. Her specialty was Polish language and literature. She knew my father had died, and kept asking to speak to my mother about our academic progress, as was customary for parent-teacher conferences four times a year. I told her the truth that our mother had passed away. She was a very good woman and provided me with a scholarship to waive my tuition fees because I had good grades. Even though my brother was one year younger than me, he had always been in the same grade as me. But Professor Ivanitska decided that he would have to be placed in the grade below me for us to both get tuition waivers (only one was allowed per grade). We were just grateful that she promised not to tell anyone that we were orphans.

Tadeusz Haska serving as an altar boy in high school in Chodzież, Poland, late 1930s.

To make money throughout high school, I continued to tutor rich kids who did not apply themselves in school. I also wrote articles in two local newspapers to make money. In the village square, my brother Antoni sold sculptures and wood carvings that he would make, and postcards that he would paint. In Chodzież there were two china factories, one for fine porcelain and one for less expensive china, that used to mold things out of gypsum. The companies would discard the old molds in a dumpsite. My brother would go there with a knife and chisel a nice piece of gypsum and make a carving out of it. He would sell the carvings to add to our household income. It is no surprise that he later became a well-known artist in Poland. We also were able to survive with the help of our local church. We served as altar boys at mass and, in return, were often given food. But it was still a great hardship to pay rent for our apartment. By the time we left for college, we had burned all the furniture in our apartment to keep warm.

My best friend was Tadeusz Kempinski. I was thrilled to find him in Bydgoszcz on my trip to Poland in 1992. Anyway, we started with forty-two students in the first year of high school, but by the third year, there were only twenty-four students left. The others had dropped out because of poor grades. During the school year 1937–1938, I reached class 8, the last class of high school. I had to take a final exam called Matura (examination of the maturity of students). It was also called Baccalaureate, and I passed the two full-day exam on May 26, 1938.

High school friends Tadeusz Kempinski and Tadeusz Haska
reunited over fifty years later in Bydgoszcz, Poland.

When I got the diploma, I felt that I was a mature man of eighteen years old. It was a very thorough and difficult exam because the courses of the entire eight years had to be taken into consideration. I had very good results in all subjects, except in mathematics I was mediocre, just satisfactory. In the last year of high school, my math professor took me to the blackboard the first day of the year and said, "Haska, if you don't apply yourself during this year, you will not pass the exam because my grade will be unsatisfactory and that will be the end of your education. You must apply yourself in math—not just in Latin, geography, literature, or Polish. If you're intelligent, you will do it. If not, too bad; that's your loss." So, from the very first day of my last year of high school, I became very serious about studying math, and I had to review eight years of this subject.

During the final exam, I was so tense that I did not believe in myself; I thought I'd probably fail, and everything would be over for me. But since I had seriously worked over the past year, suddenly when I was given the written math problems on a three-hour exam, I solved all of them in such a short time that I was sure that everything was probably wrong. The professor said, "You finished? Leave the class." I panicked and left the class, thinking I failed because everybody was still working very hard. I must have made mistakes. The best mathematicians in the class were still working and perspiring, with red faces. I finished so quickly that I thought there must be something fishy going on. The teacher forced me to leave without reviewing the problems.

A few days later, there was a celebratory ball for everyone who took the maturity test. There was an orchestra, music, fun, dancing, and a wonderful reception prepared by the students' parents. Everyone enjoyed it. When I was dancing with a female colleague, my math professor approached me and said, "Haska, you passed, and you passed the math exam with flying colors. You deserve the grade of excellent. However, you will not get it because you were lazy throughout the seven years and you only started to work this last year. On the certificate, it will only say 'good' which means B, not A. That's your punishment for being lazy for seven years." But for me, when I heard that, it was very good news. I did not care about not receiving an "excellent" in math because I received an "excellent" in all my other classes. So, I passed and was considered to be a mature person.

Passing the Matura exam entitled me to enter one of the top universities in Poland. I applied to Poznań University, which is now known as Adam Mickiewicz University, seventy kilometers south of Chodzież. I received a scholarship for tuition and free room and board, so I was very happy not having to think about food and shelter. I selected "Teacher of Polish language and literature" for my course of study in Polish Philology in order to become a high school teacher. However, if I could prove that I was able to conduct research, I could work at the university researching Slavic languages. It all depended on how I applied myself. I was a very happy student.

Meanwhile, my brother still had one more year of high school to go. Antoni stayed in our one-room apartment when I went to university in 1938. It was very hard to leave my brother, but it was unavoidable. I would visit him during vacation and holidays. He passed his maturity exam the following year when I had finished one year of university in 1939.

CHAPTER 2

The War

B y June 30, 1939, my twentieth birthday, I had an identification
document with the signatures of my professors from the entire
year for every course, certifying that I completed all the requirements
for the first year of college. On October 1, 1939, I planned to start
my second year. I arrived at Poznań one month ahead to secure
scholarships for food, meals, and student housing. Everything was
fine, except on September 1, 1939, German airplanes appeared
suddenly over the city of Poznań dropping bombs. My classmates
and I ran to the air shelter in the basement of our dormitory. We
couldn't believe what was happening. My world simply collapsed.

As soon as the bombing subsided, I immediately went to the
post office to send a letter to my brother, who had just graduated
from high school in Chodzież. He was in the process of applying to
attend the Academy of Arts in Poland. I wanted to contact him to
find out what he was planning to do. Polish guards at the post office
entrance informed me that I could not send any letters because of the
war going on. They said we were so close to the German border that
Germany already occupied the town to where I wanted to send the
letter. I was very upset and returned to my room in the dormitory.
By that time there was another air raid at noon. Again we all ran

down to the air raid shelter. There was panic everywhere. We didn't know what was going on. Polish aircraft appeared in the sky, starting a fight with German aircraft. It was only every once in a while that we saw a Polish military aircraft. My classmates and I did not understand why Poland did not seem like it was defending itself very much in the sky. We were later told that Germans had bombarded Polish airfields and destroyed much of the Polish aircraft.

Why were we attacked? Nobody could answer that. We listened to the radio, and it sounded like Hitler demanded permission from Poland to cross the Polish northern border freely from the German territory to East Prussia, a province of Germany. The Polish government responded by saying that we will not permit any transgressions of Polish territory. This caused the attack from the north, west, and south by the German army.

The situation was very difficult, and people were in a panic. Then around 4:00 or 5:00 p.m., there was another air raid and another panic and running down to the basement of the dormitory. The air raids repeated regularly every day at morning, noon, and night. I didn't know what to do, so I, together with other students, decided to try to join the Polish Army. We went to the Polish commanding general's office of armed forces in Poznań and organized a demonstration outside, shouting, "We want weapons! We want to defend our country!"

The general heard the commotion, came out on the balcony, and spoke with us. He said that Poland was attacked from too much of the west to be defended locally so the plan was to shorten the front line. He said that the Germans were only a few kilometers away from us at the time. He instructed us to go to Warsaw to report to the military commandant there to join the Polish Army. From Poznań to Warsaw it is about 300 kilometers. The only way to get there would be by train. We were instructed to wait in a nearby air raid shelter until it was close to the time of the next train's departure to Warsaw.

While waiting in the air shelter, I passed the time by making notes in an old Slavic language, trying to recall what I had learned from my previous classes. I started to write a gospel written in Old Church Slavic from the eighth or ninth century after Christ, which was a requirement for becoming a teacher of Polish. Old Church Slavic language was a foundation for Polish just like Latin was for French.

After I wrote a few lines, an officer came and asked what I was doing. I explained I was a student recalling passages from my studies. He looked at the paper and said, "You come with me."

He accused me of being a spy and asked, "What kind of letters from the alphabet are these?" Of course, these were letters from a thousand years ago. He took me to the police commander of the city of Poznań and had me arrested. Unfortunately, this would not be the only time in my life that I was arrested. The man from the air shelter presented me to some policeman and left me there as someone who was probably a spy, all because I wrote "strange signs."

I had a talk with the man interrogating me. I told him that my writings are in an old Slavic language, and he said, "Who can prove this?" I gave him the name of my professor in Poznań, Henryk Ułaszyn, who taught me this language. I told him that it was very important to me as a student of Polish language to know things relating to the curriculum. The interrogator called the professor, and the professor recalled my name and confirmed that I was his student and in his program. So, I was free! The policeman was very apologetic and bought me coffee at a restaurant--he wanted coffee too—so we went together, and he paid for my coffee and cake, and we said goodbye. This was my first experience with war. Right away, I had been accused of being a spy. I was more determined than ever to become a soldier and defend our country.

When evening approached, it was announced that everyone could leave the air shelter. I went to the railroad station and found that the train was full. I managed to get a seat on what would be the last train traveling eastward from Poznań to Warsaw. Most passengers were students and other civilians.

After we boarded, the train departed for Warsaw. Sometime

around 3:00 a.m. on September 2, 1939, the train stopped. Another bunch of airplanes dropped bombs on the train. Passengers were running away from the train, hiding in potato bushes and wherever they could find shelter. After the planes would drop bombs, they would fly very low and fire machine guns at the innocent people hiding in the bushes. Quite a few were killed. After some time, the train started moving again toward Warsaw. But in the afternoon, there was another bombing attack. Same story. Train stopped. Everyone ran away. This was repeated many times. We were bombed about three to five times every day. Once the aircraft left, the train would cautiously begin to move. The railroad tracks were unsafe, so the train had to move very slowly. We should have arrived in Warsaw in a few hours. But with the stoppages and repairs of damage to the train cars, and removing them from the tracks, it took time. So, we left on September first, but on September sixteenth we still had not made it to Warsaw. We were about halfway there in the county of Kutno.

When the bombs would approach the train, at first, I would follow the crowds running away from the train. But once I realized that a particular aircraft was right above the train, I decided not to run because I thought it would be foolish to expose myself to machine gun fire. I thought I should instead hide under the locomotive engine, full of iron to protect myself. Bombs fell near the railroad tracks, and I was fortunate because it was a swampy area so the bomb fell in the swamp and then a fountain of fragments went up into the air. One day when the bombs came, I was hiding under the locomotive, but this time a bomb was dropped very close to me. It was again a marsh area, so it exploded, and really nothing happened to me, but I felt something bothering me in my left calf. I didn't seem to be bleeding, but it hurt. Next to me, I saw a big piece of the jacket from the bomb. I thought I would keep it as a memento from the war and put it in my knapsack. The aircraft finally left, and the train started moving slowly again toward Warsaw. When evening came, my leg was so swollen that I went to see a military doctor on the train. I showed him my leg and told him that I wanted to be a soldier. He looked it over and brought back another doctor for a second opinion. After they discussed it, one of the doctors told me, "Since it is evening, we can't do anything about it. But tomorrow morning we will amputate this leg because you have an infection from a bomb fragment. If we don't amputate, gangrene will set in, and you will die. We will save your life."

I was so scared, and my friends that I met on the train were very concerned about me. I thought it over the entire night and decided that as soon as I saw some light, I would not wait for the train to depart. I would simply go to a nearby village. I decided that if I had to die, then I would prefer to die with my leg still attached. Two of my friends I met on the train wanted to leave with me. One was named Marian Konieczny, and the other one's last name was Maretski. They were not students like me, but young people who wanted to help fight in the Polish Army. Marian was a shoemaker, and I remained friends with him throughout the entire war. Not only did my friends want to help me, but they realized that the train had been bombed so many times that it was unlikely to reach Warsaw. I didn't want to run into the doctors who planned to amputate my leg, so we decided to leave the train before dawn. While everyone else was still asleep, my two friends and I left the train and walked a mile south. I could not have made the walk without their arms around me.

We arrived at the first village we could find, which was called Rdutów, and knocked on a farmer's door. It was still quite dark, so we asked him for permission to stay overnight. The very old man invited us inside and told us, "My home is already full of refugees, but you can sleep in the barn. I will bring you food." We tried to sleep for an hour or two before the sun came up. When the farmer brought us some food, he wanted to talk with us about international affairs. He asked very intelligent questions about the war situation, about Hitler, Germany, and what we thought that the Allies like France, England, the U.S., and the Soviet Union would do. He felt that farmers in Poland were exploited. When prices were low, it was hard to make a living. We agreed with most of what he was saying and discussed international affairs with him for four days. He told us that his milkman had seen some Germans and was not sure how to behave around them.

We appreciated the hospitality of the farmer, but my leg was still terribly swollen. The farmer said we should try to get medical care for me at a larger farm estate about one kilometer from his village where a farmer's wife had some medical training. In the past, she had helped many of the villagers with medical problems. With the help of my two friends, we reached the estate called Rycerzew. We reported to the owner of the estate, Mr. Zygmunt Myszkowski.

The wife was so kind. She gave me a room in the main house which felt like a palace. She invited us to dinner with her family every night. My two friends joined us the first few nights, but after that, they did not feel comfortable. They would make up some excuse why they had to eat in a different part of the estate. But because of my leg, the lady of the house simply did not permit me to go anyplace. So I was a regular guest at the table for every breakfast, dinner, and supper. She checked my leg and applied ointment every two to three hours.

The owner of the estate told me that if I wanted to return to Poznań since it was hopeless to go to Warsaw, then I should allow some time for my leg to heal first. We stayed there the entire month of October 1939. The war situation was discussed at length during meals at the table. They asked me to serve as their official translator and interpreter. Since I came from Poznań, the western part of Poland where Germany bordered Poland, they considered me an expert in German affairs and constantly asked me what would happen and what were my opinions on the situation.

I actually didn't know too much German at the time. I had learned some during the war, but in school I had studied French, Latin, and Slavic languages. But, ready or not, they brought me the newspaper and asked me to translate. The front page was usually international news, so the German words were mainly of an international nature. With the help of a German dictionary, I translated for the family at supper time the news of the day. We supplemented the information from the newspaper by listening to the radio, but it was so haphazard to be able to understand what was being said.

The family continually asked for my opinions on the war. I told them that I thought someday Hitler would be defeated, if not by Poland then by the Allies. Every day my projections looked more and more optimistic as they brought news from the neighboring towns six kilometers away that things were getting worse and worse. The only things we could hear were artillery gunfire every day and night continuously. This was both German and Polish gunfire. We established that we were hearing the gunfire from the Battle of Kutno, which was about sixty kilometers away, where the Polish defense line was. It was there where the fate of Warsaw was decided.

One day we could hear no more gunfire. We later found out that the Battle of Kutno was lost. The Germans took two weeks before the battle was decided. We also found out that the train my friends and I were on was only able to travel twenty more kilometers after we got off of it. It was forced to permanently stop in Kutno due to the battle going on there. I reasoned that because of my leg injury, I had saved myself a lot of misery by staying at the estate because Warsaw fell on September 10. The first Germans arrived, but I still had not seen them. It would not be long before I did.

My friends and I were discouraged that we could not join the Polish forces in Warsaw, but we still wanted to be a part of the underground resistance. We managed to mount some hit-and-run raids against the Nazis, but most of the time during the war, we were just trying to survive.

People often ask me how I survived World War II Poland. The short answer is that I avoided being captured by constantly changing places of living. Sometimes it was better to live in the city, other times the countryside. The real war lasted only four weeks in 1939, when Poland was attacked from all fronts. The rest of it was five years of being occupied by another country. The German government always wanted to figure out how many workers they had for each sector of the economy: iron, land, etc., and how many were educated or uneducated.

I always somehow managed not to be listed in any way because if I appeared on a list, I could be expected to be sent to work or concentration camp if they suspected I had activities against German forces. So, I tried to avoid having my name appear on any kind of lists. I succeeded in this for five and a half years. If I had gotten caught, I would have been punished by incarceration or some kind of labor camp or concentration camp or worse, hanged or shot.

I had friends who were farmers or working in the city, and I stayed with them for a while but never too long. I was like a rabbit, jumping from one hole in the ground to another, trying not to be noticed by anyone, constantly changing my place of residence.

Once I was stopped by some German policeman who demanded to know, "Where are you going?"

I said, "Home. Could you please give me a paper stating I'm going to my place of residence where I lived before the war started?"

He liked that because the German authorities wanted everyone to be in their residence from before the war. They had spies before the war started who listed people according to profession such as lawyers, teachers, and farmers in a book with their names and addresses. So when they were doing the listing, I made sure I was absent!

The reason the lists scared me so much is that if your education was high, you were the first on the list to be eliminated. Intellectuals were the number one enemy of the Third Reich. The Nazis did not like Poles to be professors, doctors, or highly educated. They were afraid of educated people who might lead the uneducated in an uprising. Polish people were only supposed to know how to count to ten and work as slave laborers. Hitler didn't care if we knew how to write because he only needed Poles to behave like working cattle. He decided that Polish people would eventually be eradicated. He wanted us to disappear from the face of the Earth so that the "Thousand-Year Reich" could extend from Russia's frontier to Japan. Anyone suspected of being a university graduate was seen as a threat and sent to a concentration camp.

I was persecuted for the fact that I had an education. I had been wearing eyeglasses since the age of thirteen. But to survive the five and a half years of German occupation, I had to hide my glasses or not wear them at all. One could also be sent to a concentration camp for nothing—just being at the wrong place at the wrong time—so it was crucial I had proper identification. When Germans were on patrol, you could be stopped, and the German would sternly say (in German): "Identification?" They would look at a Pole with glasses and say, "Aha, you are a student, teacher, or doctor; come with me." There would be a truck waiting, and they would transport you to a concentration camp, right away.

In Kraków, the German governor, Frank, ordered that all of the faculty would assemble on November 6, 1939, in one place at the university so that he could "talk to them about the future of the university." But instead, he arrested all of them and sent them to a concentration camp in Sachsenhausen-Oranienburg and Dachau, Germany, and they were never heard from again. My linguistics professor at Poznań University, Henryk Ułaszyn, was sent to a camp in Główna. The Gestapo removed the intellectuals from all the other Polish universities as well. The destiny of Poland was to be destroyed as if it had never existed.

I occasionally asked a young lady who worked in a police station cleaning the office if she saw any checklist forms lying around. She would say, "Of course." I asked for a few copies of the forms. She did it for me because we were both Poles. With these forms, I could be a salesperson or clerk using a different first name. This way, I would have something to show when I was asked for proof of my name and profession. I could hide my glasses, but I could not hide the fact that my hands were not like those of a physical laborer. Given the way the Nazis treated intellectuals, I did not want to admit that I had anything to do with a university. Clerks were still needed for the German economy, so I thought I could survive this way, and it helped me get past checkpoints on occasion.

But the most important thing that helped me survive was my knowledge of languages. I became very good at impersonating Germans. My second-grade teacher had made me memorize the Lord's Prayer in German. Whenever the German State Secret Police would question me, they demanded that I recite the prayer. Because I was able to do so in perfect German, they released me.

By October 1939, my wounded leg was healed. I still have a scar on my calf, but I am glad that I decided against surgery, especially on a train where conditions were far from suitable. My friends and I thanked our hosts at the estate and attempted to move to another area. They thought that it was not worth it for us to risk our lives by leaving, and invited us to come back anytime. The farmer said that during the First World War, things were relatively peaceful at the estate and they didn't see too many Germans in that part of Poland. They were only expected to supply Germans or Russians with grains, potatoes, fruits, and vegetables. They assumed that the same would happen for the Second World War. They would later learn the hard way that nothing could be farther from the truth.

The Soviet Union attacked from the east on September 17 and Warsaw was already taken by the Germans, so we decided to walk back to Poznań, my university town. I had left all my cold weather clothes there, and winter was quickly approaching. I was also hoping that the university was still open and I could continue my studies there. I was in the naïve frame of mind that I was a student and would be allowed to continue my studies and simply endure some hardships during the German occupation. So my friends and I returned to Poznań by walking because there was no transportation whatsoever. Railroads didn't serve civilian populations during the war. At first, we walked on the main highway, but this highway was full of German tanks, trucks, and jeeps, so it was not a very pleasant situation. We walked for three days. My first encounter with Germans was in the town of Chondiw.

Germans were all along the main highway. At first, they didn't bother us, and we didn't bother them. My friends and I walked in the area where bicycles were supposed to go. The Germans were in automobiles and didn't stop us. But when we came to Chondiw, it was full of Germans. We were walking west on a sidewalk when we encountered three or four German officers or soldiers. They were young, and I didn't know their rank. They ordered us away from the sidewalk. We did not completely understand German at the time, but we knew what they meant when they pushed us with rifles away from the sidewalk.

One of them stopped and said something in German to me: "Can you greet a German officer?"

I didn't speak perfect German, but I understood he was asking about wanting to be greeted respectfully, by taking off one's hat. I, in my lack of fully understanding German, answered him in German: "I don't understand."

It was so well-pronounced that he must have felt that I was a Polish nationalist. He thought I was too bold to not respectfully lift my hat to him. The soldier became enraged, shouting, "I'll kill you!" and grabbed his pistol to whip me or shoot me.

Being young, I ran into some house's door, ran down the hallway, then entered some other doors out the back and into some courtyard, then into a woodshed, and he ran right past me. I was safe. But I learned a valuable lesson that I should not open my mouth unnecessarily!

In all the commotion my friends spread in different directions, but we managed to find each other when we all got to the main road heading west. From that point on, we decided it was best to avoid towns. We only walked along back roads. We tried to walk at night and avoid any contact with Germans. Finally, we came to Poznań. One of my traveling companions lived in a suburb of Poznań and invited us to stay overnight with his family. It was good to finally be able to get a good night's sleep. The next day I went to the Poznań University dormitory on the avenue of Leszczynski, named after a Polish king. But I got scared when I saw German guards around it. So the first day, I didn't talk to anyone. I just walked around hoping to run into some janitors who might give me some information on what was happening with the university. I wanted to get my winter clothes out of my room.

The next day I was able to find one of the janitors from my dormitory. We went to a nearby café and talked. He said that Germans now occupied the university and had closed it. Professors had been arrested and sent to concentration camps. There was no hope that the university would ever re-open. Germans were coming and taking the apartments and houses of Poles in Poznań and taking Polish people to camps. Priests, former government officials, teachers, and educated people were among the first sent to camps. He said that there were no patterns. You never knew who would come or when someone would come to take you away. It was a scary time in Poznań. People were afraid for their lives.

I told the janitor what room I had occupied in the dormitory, and he promised to prepare a parcel containing my winter clothes. I really wanted my winter coat and long, warm underwear. We devised a plan where I was supposed to pretend that I was there to pick up the "linens" to take them somewhere. The janitor spoke German and had been a German soldier during the First World War, so the German guards tolerated him. He even wore a German cross of distinction on his uniform. The janitor gave me a piece of paper with his name on it and the office where he worked, stating that I was going to see him and instructed me to show it to the guard.

The German guard looked at the paper, grabbed me, and yelled something in German at me. He arrested me, and took me to a room and locked the door without telling me why he was doing that. I spent two hours there. When it became dark, the door suddenly opened, and a man that looked like some high-ranking officer turned the light on and looked at me. I didn't understand what he was saying, but he was shouting, full of rage. He stood at attention. Then I realized there were two men there. One was shouting at a sergeant. The sergeant then dragged me to the entrance on the street and yelled, "Go!"

I was thrilled to be released, but I did not understand what just happened. The experience frightened me, but I didn't give up on the janitor who had promised to help me. I just decided to go about it another way. I went to the coffee shop where I met him before, instead of the dormitory. I figured that he probably went there periodically for coffee breaks. When he finally showed up, he looked at me and was as pale as a white piece of paper.

He said to me, "My goodness, what happened to you? Why are you safe and not dead?"

I said, "Why should I be dead? I didn't do anything wrong."

He said, "You don't know? Earlier today they collected about twenty-five students who came back to the university, just like you, and took them to a firing range and shot them. I was sure that you were one of them!"

The janitor then figured out how it happened that I was safe. He had previously spoken to that high-ranking official whose room I was held in against my will. That official turned out to be a colonel. The janitor pretended that he didn't know me when he spoke with the colonel. The colonel had come down to the basement of the dormitory because he was in charge of headquarters.

The colonel told the janitor, "I met in my room a Polish student that was supposed to be sent to the firing squad. But when I turned on the light and looked into his eyes, I saw the eyes of my son. He looked just like my son. So I told the sergeant, this is nonsense for you to be holding this student in my room! Set him free right now."

The janitor looked at me and said, "So you see, Tadeusz, the German colonel saved you because you reminded him of his son. He told me that he hopes that someday, some stranger will spare his son's life in the same way." The janitor had not realized that I was the student that the colonel was speaking about until he saw that I was alive after the other students had been sent to be executed.

Fortunately, the friends I had been traveling with were safe. They were not former students, so they had not joined me on that day that I went to the university to try to collect my winter clothes. They invited me to stay with one of their families, but I wanted to find a way to support myself. They were nice young guys I had met on the train, but I wanted to find my old friends, my classmates. I especially wanted to reconnect with my high school girlfriend, Felicja Szuster. Her family had moved from Chodzież to Poznań. When I was a student at Poznań University, I had not bothered to get reacquainted with them because I knew I would lose a lot of time. But now seemed like the right time to go there. They received me with open arms and gave me shelter, and I spent my time thinking about what to do next.

I was actually never sure if I was Felicja's boyfriend since she had many boyfriends and I never knew if I was "the" boyfriend. Anyhow, we liked each other. My brother and I had known her since primary school. We would pretend to be her knights, and she was our queen. When we were in high school, she was an intellectual and loved to discuss world affairs. It didn't matter to me whether we were boyfriend and girlfriend or just friends. So I decided to pay her and her family a visit. It wasn't easy to find them because they had changed homes. They now lived in a beautiful two-story home that was owned by their physician uncle at 7 Reymonta Street in Poznań. When I knocked on the door, they took me to their part of the home, which was in the basement.

The uncle had brought his family out of the country when the war started and offered his house for them to live in because they were previously living in an apartment in a part of town that had become dangerous during the German occupation. The father of my girlfriend was smart. He moved the family downstairs in the basement because he knew that German civilian families would occupy the upstairs. When Germans took over the home, they allowed this family to stay below as caretakers and janitors. This man adapted very easily to his position as janitor because he knew what the Germans were capable of.

When the Germans took over Polish people's homes, if they did not go to a concentration camp, they had to move to an area of German occupation called General Government (GG). The only Polish people allowed to stay were those with German roots, German names, or jobs working for new German settlers. Felicja's parents spoke German well, so they were allowed to remain in the basement of their home, in the renamed area called Warthegau, which the Germans considered part of their country. If the Polish people living there wanted to go to GG, where most Poles were, they would have to ask for passes, which were rarely approved.

Felicja's family invited me to stay with them, but after I learned what happened in Poznań of people dying every day, I didn't want to stay. There were no Jews in Poznań, but the Germans wanted to kill the educated people and Catholics, not just the Jews. When I decided to leave Poznań, I contacted my other friends from the train, but one of them, Maretski, preferred to stay in Poznań. The other one, Marian the shoemaker, was ready to go with me, but when I got to where he was staying, he wasn't there. They told me that he had been looking for me where I was staying, but unfortunately, we must have just missed one another.

I wanted a traveling companion, so I contacted another high school friend, and he agreed that leaving the country with me to join the Polish forces in an Allied country would be best. We had heard over the radio that there was a Polish government in exile where we could join the Polish Army in one of those countries and fight the Germans there. A few days later, he and I bought used bicycles and decided to leave the country through the southern border of Poland. From there we would go to Hungary or Romania and then to France and join the Polish forces in France.

My friend and I went to a German military commander's office because many refugees were returning to their homes. We asked for a paper stating that we were returning home. I had no intention of going "home" because I had no home due to the closing of my university. But I thought that if I got the certificate, it would allow me to travel south without suspicion. Whenever they stopped me, I showed the document, and they said: "OK, go home."

But before going anywhere, we decided to make some money because how can you go someplace and expect to get shelter and food without paying for it? At that time, there were shortages of practically everything. My friend was the son of a merchant in Chodzież, and he bragged that he had the gift of how to make money. He told me that his brother lived in the industrial city of Łódź, second in size to Warsaw at the time, southwest of Poznań, working as a manager in a textile factory. My friend said his brother would give us textiles such as socks or silk stockings to sell in villages. It would allow us to make a quick buck, and then we could have enough money to leave the country. We decided to travel to my friend's brother on bicycles. But how would we make it there without being arrested by the Nazis for being Polish partisans or intellectuals? Once again, I had to remove my glasses to disguise my education. Otherwise, I would immediately have been shot.

Thankfully we made it to Łódź on our bicycles. That is where we saw Polish Jews for the first time. They were not yet segregated. But we knew they were Jews because the Nazis forced all Jews to wear a yellow star of David on their clothing—on their breasts and their backs. There were signs all over Poland that stated that it was a law that all Jews must wear the Star of David. At the time, I thought this was a terrible persecution, but I did not realize yet how dangerous the situation was for them. The Nazis wanted it to be easy to identify a Jew so that they could quickly punish them for doing something wrong. For example, when it was decided that Jews had to walk on the street and not the sidewalk, then they could easily identify which people on it were Jews breaking the law. Even without the Stars of David, it was easy to distinguish some Jews on the street because orthodox Hasidic Jews wore special robes and some Jews used Yiddish to communicate. But other Jews would not have been distinguishable without the Star of David on their clothing.

One thing that I realized from this experience as a young man is that you cannot tell if someone is Jewish simply by looking at them. I had thought that I would have been able to tell by their dress, language, or facial features. But when I saw how many people wore a star of David, it became clear to me that many of these people looked just like the non-Jew Poles I knew, and I would not have known that they were Jews if they were not wearing a Star of David. It is interesting that Jews had been living in Poland since the thirteenth century, but there were different degrees of assimilation. Some had chosen to give their babies Polish first names and even added "ski" to the end of their last names, while other Polish Jews had kept more of their Jewish culture. It was tragic that the second group were more likely to be rounded up and forced to live in ghettos or killed in concentration camps.

The Nazis wanted to divide Polish society into two groups: non-Jews and Jews. They hoped Poles would enjoy joining the Germans in persecuting the Jews. It did not work. Poles were not Germans, and Poles were persecuted too. Poles realized that it was just a matter of time before the Germans would annihilate everyone: first the Jews, then the Poles. Jews were a minority in Poland, so the Germans decided to kill them first.

But at that time, we did not know that the Germans were planning to kill the Jews. We only thought that they were trying to punish them. Nazi propaganda spread lies that the Jews were to blame for the war. Hitler said that if it were not for the Jews, then France and England would not have declared war on Germany after he attacked Poland. He said that the Jews incited the governments of France and England to declare war on Germany. Jews were in fact persecuted in Germany for six years from 1933 to 1939 before Hitler even attacked Poland. I was flabbergasted that the Jews were being targeted. I had initially thought that Germany was only occupying Poland militarily.

When we arrived in Łódź, my friend's brother gave us textiles. We took them to sell in the countryside and returned to Łódź with money to get more textiles to sell and continued this process several times. It may seem unbelievable that we were able to travel like that during the war. As I mentioned, it was announced in every part of Poland that every Pole must return to his place of residence before the war. So we went to the German military commander's office and were given another piece of paper stating our name and that we should be helped to get to our place of residence because we were the good guys following the rules. This paper enabled us to travel. Before the war, the Germans prepared by making lists of where Poles lived and who should be arrested and taken to a concentration camp in the future, for example, for belonging to a Polish nationalist organization. The Germans found it frustrating that the Polish lists were in flux because people were always changing their residences. So that's why they required people to go home to where they were at the start of the war and decided it was in their best interest to help refugees make it home.

But I instead decided that I would use the paper to keep moving around, all the while pretending to go home. Whenever we were stopped, we would tell the German officials that we were the good guys going home like we were told. The Germans would say, "Good, go home." So we used that paper to travel back and forth, selling textiles to the countryside. At some point, I thought we had enough money to leave the country and join the Allied forces, but my friend was a bit greedy and wanted to continue selling for a little while longer, and I reluctantly agreed. Unfortunately, that was a mistake because by the time we decided we had enough money to leave the country, it was too late!

When we arrived at a village near the border of Hungary, it was well-guarded and completely sealed off. It was November 1939 now and Germans had attacked from the south, north, and west. People told us that if you dared to approach within 100 kilometers of the border or asked about someone who lived on the other side of the border, you would be arrested, sent away, and never heard from again. We then planned to get to German-occupied Czechoslovakia but discovered that it was too late. Because of the time wasted from healing my injured leg, I could not have come sooner.

My friend and I decided it would be best to wait for a better time to approach the border. At that time it was winter 1939. Snow fell, and we couldn't ride our bicycles in the deep snow. But fortunately, I had my winter clothes thanks to the kind janitor from my university. But my traveling companion friend got sick with the flu and wanted to stay with his brother. I rode north on my bicycle so that I could go back to the farmer's estate, where I had stayed at the beginning of the war. This was a journey that I will never forget. For the first time during the war, I was traveling alone. It was snowing so heavily that I could barely see. I had to walk and drag my bicycle. I was so tired that I wanted to sit down, but I remembered that my father told me that when it was snowing and there was frost and you were tired, you should not stop for any reason because you would fall asleep and never wake up. So I kept walking and walking and walking and knocked on the door of some farmer's home, asking for shelter. They provided me food and were very nice to me. The next morning, the farmer urged me to stay one day longer. But I was determined to keep going, so I walked, all the while pushing my bicycle, another day and then another day, and on the third day, I finally reached that estate where I had stayed earlier in the war with my shoemaker friend. I was grateful for the farmer's wife healing my wounded leg.

When I arrived, the farmer and his family welcomed me with open arms. They told me that my shoemaker friend, Marian Konieczny, had already been back to see them.

He had settled in the nearby village of Rdutów and opened a shoe repair shop. He had a girlfriend, but they never married. From this point on, I visited him often, and we would always discuss international affairs. He made me a special pair of wool boots that shined like officers of the Polish Army would wear. They were beautiful and fit me perfectly. We became very close friends.

Sadly, after the war, he went to Berlin on business—buying or selling leather for his shoes—and never made it home. A Soviet soldier killed him. After the war, it was very difficult to travel, but I managed to visit Marian's siblings near Poznań to find out what happened to him. He used to travel to Berlin regularly as part of his shoe business. Later it was reported that the Soviet soldiers killed him because they said he was in some place that he was not supposed to be.

I was invited to stay at the Rycerzew estate and serve as an interpreter as I had at the beginning of the war. German newspapers were arriving, and in the evening supper time, they wanted to be able to hear the latest news. I met a few refugees like me there, but by that time, most had returned to their place of origin. The owner of the estate who had sheltered me at the beginning of the war, Mr. Myszkowski, introduced me to the administrator of the estate who was helping him manage it, Zygmunt Sokołowski. Both of these men had graduated from university with a degree in agriculture. I was treated just like a member of the family. They were very interested in hearing from me what I saw and what was happening during the war.

I told the family my experiences with the Nazis and the horrible things that they were doing to the Poles and Jews. But after a while, I noticed that the family would listen politely but then say, "Yes, of course, we remember from the First World War when Germany attacked Belgium, on the French side there were horrible stories of violence of Germans against the Belgian population, but these were only partly true." They discounted certain things as the Allies' propaganda against Germans. In other words, my hosts were politely trying to tell me that they were hearing what I was telling them, but that they know some Germans who were civilized people. They told me, "The Allies are probably exaggerating the extent to which Germans are engaging in atrocities. Germans didn't bother us during the First World War, and we hope that they will not bother us during this war. We hardly noticed that there is a war. Everything seems to be civilized."

When my hosts did not believe me, this made me very unhappy. I said to them, "You do not believe me? I was running to the county seat town of Chludowo in the province of Poznań. I was stopped in the center marketplace by a terrible scene. There were a huge amount of German soldiers who ordered Polish citizens to gather in a certain area. They were then forced to watch the execution of 30 prominent citizens of the town instructed to stand against a wall of sandbags in front of a firing squad. When passersby started to leave with their families, they were forced to stand there for several hours. The goal was to terrify these people so that they would not lift a finger against the Germans. I was so scared that I left that town as quickly as possible."

My hosts at the estate shook their heads and said, "Yes, but maybe they were not shot; maybe they were just hostages."

I told them, "No, I watched these innocent people murdered by the German soldiers."

They said, "You are young and probably hate Germans."

I told them that I had watched the Germans take over Poznań methodically, section by section. Instead of taking over the entire city in one day, they systematically chose fifteen-block areas each day where they would enter houses, tell innocent Poles to leave everything they had except for one small suitcase, and board a bus for Łódź so the Germans could classify them. If they were old, they were sent to Warsaw. The young were sent to Germany for forced labor in factories or farms, and the educated were sent to concentration camps for certain death. I had watched this with my own eyes in Poznań.

I decided that it would be my job to open these people's eyes to the reality of the war. It turned out that someone else would be the one to show them the harsh truth of what was happening.

One evening in April 1940, when I was translating German news at the supper table, trucks arrived at the estate. They took the owner and his wife to a concentration camp, not yet for killing but for trying to figure out what to do with them. A German administrator right away took over their estate. I decided it was not safe for me to be there, so I quickly fled to a nearby village. A Polish farmer offered me some shelter and food if I'd teach the children because all schools were closed in the entire country.

I had not met my wife Jadwiga yet, but she was fifteen years old when the war began. She had attended one of the illegal "secret schools" in Poland at someone's home called complets. Secret school was held at a different home each week to be discreet. It was punishable by death or concentration camp to attend one of those schools, but her parents valued education, and Jadwiga did not want to stop learning after the war started.

The only objective at the time was survival. There was no entertainment. All movies, opera, theater, etc. were closed. Anyone on the streets after 6:00 p.m. would be shot by Germans. Jadwiga's beloved grandpa, Tomasz Borzym, had been killed by the Germans for being outside after the curfew. After his death, she had nightmares from witnessing the Germans setting people on fire in the streets of Warsaw.

I stayed there for a while with the farmer, trying to figure out what to do next. I could not show the "going home" certificate anymore because the date on it was expired. I knew that I had to disappear from the area because I had already unknowingly created some suspicion.

One day, while walking, I was stopped by a German policeman who accused me of being some agent of the underground since I didn't look like other farmers. I had made the mistake of wearing my eyeglasses. He said that he would "take care of me!" I did not look like the workers because I had glasses, which meant I knew how to read books, so they thought I might be organizing an underground resistance. As a result, I was arrested by a regular German policeman.

But when he took me to jail, the chief looked like a decent man. I found out he came from Austria, not Germany. He asked why I was arrested. I said that I did not know. For some unknown reason, he set me free. I believe that, because he was an Austrian, he may not have agreed with whatever the Germans were doing. Now I was safe, but now what should I do? It was only a matter of time before this would happen again.

I was determined to find a place where I could survive the war. In cities like Poznań, it would be extremely difficult because cities were invaded by German settlers who occupied everything belonging to Poles—businesses, factories, housing, and so on. Polish families were shocked when the Germans came while they were eating supper. The Germans would say, "This is our place now; you must leave and cannot take anything with you because we now are taking everything you own." Polish families were sent places such as a large industrial center where, in the factories, they awaited selection by the Gestapo (German State Secret Police). I decided being sent to a farm would be the best way to survive. There would be enough food, unlike in cities.

I went to a newly established office that set up jobs for Polish people to work in the German economy in Poland or Germany in factories, farms, etc. In this office, both Germans and Poles were working. I asked a woman working there if she would send me to a farm in East Prussia. It was a gamble. In East Prussia, I knew there was a province called Warmia, where people spoke Polish because it used to be a Polish province. My mother's ancestors came from there. Before 1939, it was a German province inhabited by German citizens who were of Polish descent. They spoke Polish and were Catholics who maintained their patriotism toward everything Polish. If I could be sent there, I would have a good time with Polish farmers. It was not certain that I would find a Polish family there, so it was a gamble; but I would prefer that gamble to being shot by another policeman thinking I'm a spy.

Luckily, they sent me by train to an assignment in East Prussia in the village of Skajboty, and I found myself knocking on a farmer's door. A letter introduced me to Jozef Kellmann as his new farmhand. Kellmann was a German name, and when I introduced myself, he spoke to me in German. I could not speak German well at the time, so I spoke in Polish, and he answered in Polish! I could not believe my good fortune.

His father standing nearby spoke Polish, and told his son, "Grab him, he's a Pole; let's help him." The father then said to me in Polish, "I don't speak German at all either, even though I'm ninety years old and live in a German province!"

The German son switched to Polish, and we talked. I said, "This is a very good occasion that I'm sent to you. I won a big lottery of life!" I laughed. Right away, they became my friends. Whenever I was not working, and especially at mealtimes, we'd talk in Polish about Poland, Polish history, and how I found myself in a Polish home. I was very lucky. I learned how to work on a farm, and I was pleased that I was able to work and get acquainted with the farm business. Even if the war lasted several years, there would be enough food, and recreation, and the sun was shining. It was a pleasant situation I found myself in. I thought that no matter how long this war lasted, I would survive.

I was delighted to receive two postcards from my high school girlfriend, Felicja Szuster, while working at Kellmann's farm.

Tadeusz Haska working at the farm estate of Jozef Kellmann
in Skajboty, Poland in 1940.

I ended up staying there for eleven months. Kellmann and the other farmers had French prisoners of war as farmhands. At that time, it was 1940, and France was somehow beaten in four weeks, just like Poland. I did not understand how it could have happened so quickly. It was a great disappointment to all Poles. In Poland, we had thought that France would show Hitler what war was since they had defeated Germany in World War I. We had thought France would show Hitler that it is not worth it to start a war.

I had heard that French soldiers did not want to fight. They threw down their rifles and did not resist. When I met the French prisoners of war, I asked them, "Why didn't you fight? Why are you here? You remember 1914 and 1918 when France was victorious and won the First World War? Now you gave up and surrender?" I knew how to speak French well. They were very ashamed and said that they had been listening to Radio Moscow in French. One of them explained, "We were opposed to Hitler; however, Moscow told us not to fight and then there would be no war."

Now the French prisoners found themselves in a situation where they did not understand German. Farmers sent for me to interpret for them. Before I had arrived, when the German farmers would tell the French prisoners to do something, the French prisoners would respond in French, "I don't know," as they shrugged their shoulders, and just stood there. The German farmers needed me to give the French prisoners their job instructions. The French were peaceful; they weren't revolting, but they just needed to be told what to do in their own language. Now some knew what to do but pretended that they did not. But others came from industrial parts of France and truly did not know how to farm. I was the only one in the area who knew French except for the prisoners of war, so I quickly became popular with not only my farmer but the neighboring farmers, who often asked me to translate job orders to their French workers.

I became close friends with three of the French prisoners of war in particular. On my birthday, they gave me a pipe and pouch of pipe tobacco. This was the only time in my life that I tried smoking, but I actually only pretended to smoke so that I did not offend them. These French workers used their pipe smoking as a pretext to take regular breaks from working. It bothered them to watch me do their jobs while they took a break, so that is why they gave me the pipe as a gift. I pretended to smoke, taking care not to inhale, so that I could be in solidarity with the Frenchmen.

Everything was fine, except after eleven months I was forced to make another life-changing decision. It was harvesting time in 1940. Farmers in that area of Warmia who were Polish or German invited other farmers to help them out because harvest required a lot of workers to get the grains into the barn and house, etc. One day, a neighbor farmer had a harvest. My farmer and I, as his farmhand, were asked to help. All the other farmers in the vicinity did the same thing. As usual, I was also needed to translate job orders to the French workers. At lunchtime, my farmer and I were invited to the farmhouse to eat with the neighbor farmer and his wife. Since I was used as an interpreter, the wife of the farmer invited me to the dining room to eat with other farmers while the French prisoners of war were in the kitchen eating lunch. I thanked her for the offer but said I'd prefer to stay with my people, the French prisoners, in the kitchen. The lady was very upset that I refused to eat with them, but I felt an obligation to eat with my fellow workers.

After lunch, we returned to work. There was a huge harvesting machine. Everything worked okay, except after a half hour there was a huge noise. There was a terrible crash from the machine, and it stopped. We were sent home. I later heard that somebody dropped a stone or piece of rock into the machine, and that's why everything broke inside, and we could not return to work since it did not work anymore. It was considered sabotage. A French prisoner of war on top of the machine threw the rock material in there. He was not considered guilty because he said that I told him to put the rock in there to sabotage the German economy! I did no such thing, but my farmer informed me that this would be a very ugly affair.

In the evening, a policeman came to my farmer and told him that he would be arresting me and sending me to a concentration camp for sabotage. My farmer invited him to the dining room, gave him supper, and poured him a lot of Schnapps whiskey. The policeman became so drunk that he decided to arrest me the next morning instead of that evening. Before he left, my farmer gave him a big ham for his wife in Berlin. She probably needed some food, given the food shortages. My farmer approached me and said, "You probably know what you must do. I am going to be absent from the farm for three days to harvest hay in a distant village." So, he was giving me the green light to escape. Disappear.

And so that's what I did. But I did not go on foot, because I was afraid that if I did, someone would see me wandering and arrest me in a few hours, either to prison or a concentration camp or whatever. Many Poles tried to escape by simply walking away from the place they worked, but none of them succeeded. So, I developed a different plan. I went to the local railroad station and borrowed my farmer's hat with a little feather in it. I approached the window where railroad tickets were sold. My knowledge of languages helped me here. I pretended to be a German soldier, making certain noises with the boots I was wearing and in the way that I walked. There was a girl selling the tickets. I requested a first-class ticket to Berlin. The way I said it was in a very sure, stern German voice, *ordering* her to get me a first-class trip to Berlin. She meekly accepted my money and gave me a ticket without asking me for proof of permission by the police for buying a ticket. She thought I was a German. Of course, I had no intentions of going to Berlin. I just wanted a ticket, and from East Prussia, I would travel through Poland and stop in Poznań, which was on the way to Berlin.

After boarding the train, I asked the first-class compartment conductor not to disturb me because I wanted to sleep. I gave the conductor a twenty and asked him to wake me up when we arrived in a large city so that I could buy a newspaper. He was happy to accommodate me. I was careful to say simply "large city" and not mention the name of the city Poznań, but I knew it would be Poznań. The reason I bought a first-class ticket was that I knew that in the first-class compartment, I'd be all alone. I did not know enough German to be in a conversation if I was in third class. People would eventually start asking questions, and I'd be discovered as a non-German not allowed to travel, and I'd be prevented from escaping. Most people traveled third or second class. Traveling in the first-class compartment meant that nobody would ask me any questions.

The conductor woke me up in Poznań, and I left the train with no intention of returning. When I went to "buy the newspaper," this was simply a ruse. I just wanted to get off the train without being noticed by the police who were standing near the newsstand. I went straight to visit my high school girlfriend, Felicja, and her family in Poznań. I remembered their address because I had been corresponding with Felicja. I stayed there for two to three months until I was able to secure some identification.

I tried to read German newspapers to find a word in the countryside far from Poznań. I found an announcement that some German administrator sent from Germany to Poland to administer a large estate, Chodów, in the village Rdutów in the county of Kutno, located halfway between Poznań and Warsaw. I wrote a letter offering my services as an interpreter of Polish and German. Three days later, I received a telegram from that administrator accepting my request for a position and asking me to come to introduce myself.

So I went to the railroad station, using the telegram as official permission to travel, legitimately this time, and went to the Chodów estate, which was formerly owned by a Polish senator. When the war had broken out, he had moved to Warsaw, because he had anticipated that the estate would be taken over by Germans and had not wanted to face them.

When I arrived, I introduced myself to a gentleman in a German lieutenant uniform named Karl Thieme, who instructed me to be his bookkeeper and interpreter. I still did not feel that I knew German very well, but I was able to bluff. I started to read German newspapers and studied German on my own from a textbook. Pretty soon, I was able to function as an interpreter to the other Polish employees, and I dictated letters to the German commissar. He was a reasonable man. In Germany, he had been the owner of an estate, and he had just been sent by the German army to take over a Polish estate. I met his wife, and they were very nice people to me. After a few months, this lieutenant, who had been in the reserves, was sent to the front lines, and soon after his wife received a notice that he was killed in Russia.

After his death, another German commissar, named Robert Maltzan, took over the estate. He was not a farmer and had no idea what administration of an agricultural estate entailed. He had been a waiter from a hotel in Hamburg, and the only preparation that he had for such a position was that he was a member of Hitler's Nazi party. He had no education and behaved like a terrorist. He only gave orders to the Polish administrator. Still, he was not looking for any kind of trouble. He wanted the farm to produce as much food as possible for the German economy. Maltzan did not want to lose any workers, so he protected us from being sent to Germany by the German police.

The scary part was that he often hosted receptions for all kinds of Nazi party members, including the Gestapo. He was trying to get on good terms with them. But when I would see the Gestapo arrive at the estate with their guns, I would grab a blanket and sleep on a bench in the park. I spent many nights like that. I did not realize that they were simply coming to visit Maltzan on friendly terms. I thought that maybe Maltzan had called them to arrest me, and I didn't want them to find me in my room, so I slept on a bench whenever they came over. I stayed at that farm until the end of the war. There was enough food, but Maltzan did not know how to speak in a normal tone of voice. He always was yelling and tried to cover up what he did not know about farming by yelling orders.

While working there, I received seventy-two postcards from Felicja. The Arbeitsamt forcibly assigned her to work as a secretary at the Focke-Wulf factory where Germany built aircraft during the war. She was forced to work such long hours that when she went to work in the morning, it was dark, and it was dark when she returned home at night. She hated it there and requested to be reassigned, but they refused to allow her to leave. Felicja wrote about learning shorthand. It was so cold there that she got frostbite on her fingers, and had trouble writing the Gothic letters she was required to write. She said that the work was very difficult, and there were a lot of "bad people" all around her. She disliked being forced to work on Sundays. Eventually, the factory put her in a new job teaching German there, which she liked better. She wrote that her boss later committed suicide.

After the war, Felicja told me that she provided a map of the Focke Wulf factory to a British spy named Zucker during the war. Officially he was called Volksdeutsche, and he came from time to time to Focke-Wulf as a seller, all the while collaborating with two Poles working in the factory. Near the end of the war, the Gestapo entered the factory and arrested one of the Polish spies. While trying to escape, the Pole bit the Gestapo man in the finger. The Gestapo came to the office, very angry, telling Felicja to get him a bandage, and that's how she found out what had happened. The Gestapo thought that only Germans were working there, so he did not realize that Felicja was a Pole. At that time the second Polish spy was in Krzesiny, just outside the city, at another location of the factory at the air force base where new machines were tested. After the Gestapo left, Felicja went to the telephone central and asked a telephonist to call Krzesiny and tell the second Pole that his partner had been arrested. This allowed the second spy enough time to escape.

In her postcards, Felicja informed me that she had to move my belongings from our friend Zofia Kaminska's home to her family's flat. Sadly Zofia was killed by the Gestapo in Warsaw. Felicja also wrote about her desire to be free from her possessive fiancé, Bogdan Firlej. But her work was causing her so much stress that she longed to get married soon and be free from her job so that she would not "become a hysteric." She eventually broke off the engagement with Bogdan and also broke one off with a nice man named Kornel Michalowski. She married Kazimierz Mieczysław Blicharski, five days after they met. Felicja's father and brother, Hen, were forcibly taken away by the Germans to dig fortifications around Poznań. Fortunately, they were allowed to return home after a month or two. Felicja would often ask about my opinion on the Russian Army, using code words, of course, so that the postcard would not be censored. She sometimes wrote fake letters to me about everything being fine, just to please the censors.

The end of the war came, and I overheard the Germans making some plans of destruction. They were planning to lock people in buildings, schools, and churches and create some underground explosions. But the Soviet army came so quickly that the Germans didn't have time to carry out their plan of destruction, and somehow I survived. Trucks arrived with Soviet soldiers to announce the end of the war. One Soviet political officer climbed out of the truck and told all of the Polish workers to assemble in one area, and listen to his speech.

Another officer went, one by one, to each Polish worker, and asked him, "What time do you have?" When the worker would look at his watch, the officer would force the worker to give him the watch. When he came to me, I pretended not to understand. My watch was in my inside pocket, so he did not even realize that I had one. He collected all of the rest of the watches, putting them in the truck.

The other officer giving the speech shouted, "We are liberating all of you from the Germans now."

And a few of the workers responded, "And from our watches!"

My brother Antoni also managed to survive the war. He was forcibly sent to work by the Arbeitsamt. For the first three years, he worked as a farm worker in the village of Swoboda in central Poland. For the remaining years of the war, he was sent to the estate of Witow in southern Poland.

CHAPTER 3

After the War

Marriage, Jail, and Life as a Refugee

W hen the war ended in 1945, I left the estate Chodów and went back to my university town of Poznań. I hoped to enter the university, but the school was in the process of re-organizing itself to get rid of all German changes imposed. The university had been closed for five years, so there was a lot of work to be done. I went to a Polish Western Union organization and asked for a job in the regained territories. Poland regained western territories, and the border was now on a river where I got an assignment to the town Derlow, which is now known as Darłowo. It was a beautiful little coastal town on the Baltic Sea that was not destroyed by any German or Soviet war actions. The Polish population started returning, and the Germans started going back to Germany.

First there was a center of German command; when they left, the Soviet army moved in and again it was a seat of a Soviet Russian commanding general. So I reported to the mayor, Stanisław Dulewicz, who had previously been a professor. He was forcibly sent by Germans to work in Germany during the war. When he was liberated, he was elected mayor of the town. Since he had previously been a professor, he dreamed of organizing a Polish high school and junior college in this town. Although he was mayor, he also became director of the junior college. He offered me two jobs. During the daytime, I helped reestablish Polish administration of the town and even officiated at some weddings. In the evening, I was a teacher of Polish language and literature, Latin, and French. I worked twelve- to fourteen-hour days, but I was very happy. The students who enrolled in this junior college were young people who lost a lot of time because of the duration of the war (5 ½ years). They were very eager to study, and it was a real pleasure to teach them.

During the time I was teaching in Derlow, I met my future wife, Jadwiga. Her parents named her after Saint Jadwiga (1174-1243) and Queen Jadwiga (1373-1399). When I saw her at a concert in Derlow, it was love at first sight. She was there with her friend Danka, and I was there with my friend, who was a priest. During the intermission at the concert, I went over to Jadwiga and introduced myself.

Two days later, I sent her roses and a letter asking for a date. It was nearly impossible to get flowers in Poland in September 1945, so I made quite an impression on her. Whenever I would bring her flowers throughout our fifty-seven-year marriage, it always brought a smile to her face.

I proposed on a bridge over the river Wieprza under the light of the moon. I told her that she would always have everything she needed, but that I was not someone to chase after money.

Our wedding on September 18, 1946, was tiny and quiet. Because I belonged to the anti-Communist political party, I needed to keep a low public profile. Only my brother, Antoni, attended the wedding.

Even though I was a teacher, Jadwiga's parents were skeptical of me for a while. They were from Warsaw, a big city, and saw me as a peasant boy from the countryside. There were even prejudices about eye color. City dwellers in Poland like Jadwiga's parents were more likely to have brown eyes and Polish people in the countryside were more likely to have blue eyes. Jadwiga's mother, in particular, was distrusting of my blue eyes. My mother-in-law was also concerned that my work as a member of the Polish underground resistance movement during the war would put Jadwiga in danger. When Jadwiga moved into my home, she and her mother were horrified to find grenades in the china cabinet and rifles under the bed. They were so terrified that they secretly buried the weapons in the backyard. At that time, possession of weapons was met with immediate execution.

I wrote the letter below to Jadwiga while traveling two months before our wedding.

Poznań, 21 July 1946

My Jadzia!

I was a witness today of a scene which for the Poznań residents was something jubilant to their hearts. Today at 7:00 in the morning Geiser was hanged. You as a Warsaw resident surely do not know who Greiser was. Here in greater Poland every child knows Greiser. He was a Great Poland executioner, Hitler's governor, Gauleiter, Reichsstatthalter. He devastated the greater Poland intelligentsia, the clergy; he turned the Polish people into labor cattle (Arbeitsvieh). Today he dangled so innocently on gallows. I was just five meters away from him. He was laid in a coffin—one of those which survived in the famous prison at Młynarska where the corpses of Polish convicts were laid. The gallows were placed on a hill, so it was visible from a great distance. There were incredible crowds of people around the hill. Just after 6:00 in the morning there were races at the streets of cars, bikes, and motorbikes to make it to the execution. Before 7:00, the streets were full— everyone was running to the Poznań citadel where the gallows stood as if they were to put out a fire. Greiser was hanged in silence. He hanged for 20 minutes. For you. this surname is like any German person's surname. The Poznań mothers lifted their children up high to show them the dangling dead body saying: "Look, he's Greiser the executioner! He murdered your father, your brother died because of him! When you grow up to be a man, a father, then you could say that justice was done, the Greiser the murderer was punished!" The crowds were quiet until laying Greiser in the coffin. Then everyone ran up to see the dead body. They were swearing everywhere. The women in particular forgot themselves and were showing their hate with swearing.

How are you? I am staying in Poznań as firstly I need to take my shoes and secondly, I have coffee that I need to sell as I am running out of money. Soon I'll be in Derłowo. Have you received my letters and postcards? I sent a few. In the meantime, I send my love to you. You surely have forgotten about me, eh? How is your leg? Apparently, the mosquitos in Derlow show no mercy!

Love, Tad

Tadeusz and Jadwiga's home in Derlow, Poland.

Jadwiga and I lived in a big, beautiful house, and everything was ideal. It was really a pleasure to teach and to live in that little town, until something happened. Namely, the Soviet Secret Police opened an office in Derlow. They had a building in the marketplace, and right away, all kinds of unpleasant things started to happen.

While working at the junior college, I was very active in government affairs. The curator of the local castle, Amelia Łączyńska, and I founded the Polish People's Party (also known as the Polish Peasants' Party or Polskie Stronnictwo Ludowe; PSL) in Derlow. I served as secretary of the national municipal council representing the PSL.

The Communists wanted to liquidate my party. The name of the party members translated to English as "people who live in the countryside." Most of the Polish population belonged to that party even though they had nothing to do with farming, but they supported the prime minister and his peasant party. Friends persuaded me to run for Parliament in the January 1947 elections that were supposed to be "free and unfettered." They wanted me to serve as their Derlow district candidate to represent them in Warsaw. I accepted their nomination, but it wasn't a very sound decision from the standpoint of my safety.

The first city board meeting of 1946 in Derlow, Poland.
Tadeusz Haska is in the first row, third from left.

I received warnings that if I didn't drop this idea of belonging to a party opposing Communism, it would be disastrous for me because I would be put in prison. But these were just rumors. The threats came from the commandant of the Secret Police. People were coming to me and telling me to be careful because the Communists would not let me go to Warsaw. But I was young and full of energy, and I decided that I could not be scared. Most people I knew were on my side, so I disregarded the warnings.

But I was naïve. Soviet troops were occupying Poland! Stalin was alive at the time, and the Communist Party would never let the opposition win the election. Before elections could take place in January, they arrested me in December. It was a preventive arrest so that I would not be able to campaign for this seat. I guess the Communists figured that no one would vote for me if I were in jail.

On December 7, 1946, I was in my office at the junior college when two soldiers with rifles arrived and told me that the Commandant of the Soviet Secret Police, Zdzisław Kowalski, wanted to talk to me. I tried not to go, but they said they would be forced to use their rifles if necessary. So I went.

The chief of the Soviet Secret Police was very pleasant at first. I said that everyone knew that he was from the Department of Security and he started by asking me if I owned, before the war, any factories, or if I was a capitalist with a large agricultural estate, or whether I was a banker. I answered him emphatically, "No. I am a working person. I am a teacher."

He said, "Then why are you on the other side? Why are you not with us? You are one of us. You should be on our side, the side of the workers." What he meant was the side of the Communist Party.

I told him, "I'm not going to change my political affiliation because I want Poland to be Poland, not a Soviet republic." I explained that I wanted to make sure that Poland would be free from any interference from other powers.

The Commandant was very angry with me and told me that he was going for dinner to a restaurant with another person sent from Warsaw to help get rid of people like me. He said that he hoped that I would change my mind by the time that he would return from dinner.

As soon as the Commandant left, a soldier entered the room and quickly opened a trap door in the floor and pushed me down the hole into a basement. The soldier informed me that he was instructed to let me out at midnight when the Commandant would come back.

I found myself in a dark space with water almost up to my knees. When I tried to stand up, I could not because there was not enough room, so I had to crouch. I understood that this was done to me to try to get me to change my mind when he returned from dinner. It was so uncomfortable. I was not very happy, of course. I thought, *How long am I going to have to stay here?* It was 8:00 in the evening. At midnight, the door opened, and the soldier took me out of the hole and told me that any minute the commandant would be back. He instructed me to sit on the chair in the commandant's office to wait for the commandant's return.

I knew I had been down in the cellar for four hours because the clock in the city hall tower was chiming very loudly once every half hour. It had sounded eight times since I had been down there. While waiting, I looked around the office and noticed that a man was asleep on a couch.

He was snoring, but when he woke up and looked up, he said, "Who are YOU?"

I said, "What about you? Who are you?"

He said, "Don't worry, I'm just a bailiff from a village here. I killed two Russian soldiers, but I'm not worried because I'm a member of the Communist party. A Polish woman who owns a farm called me for help in stopping some Russian soldiers from stealing a cow from her farm. I shot and killed the thieves when they refused to return the cow. Nothing will happen to me because I am a member of the Communist party. Those two soldiers were deserters, so I was justified in killing them for stealing the cow. I will just sign a report, and I will be free. I'm just waiting for the commandant to return.

"But *you* are in trouble. Isn't your name Haska? I heard someone on the phone, and your name was mentioned. The Soviet Secret Police commandant said you are supposed to be transported to the next county seat town where there is a prison. You better disappear before morning."

I was afraid that he was trying to talk me into escape and that while I was escaping, they would try to kill me. I thought he was a provocateur. Then he fell asleep and started snoring again. I was scared of doing something foolish. But when I heard the tower chime signaling that it was 1:00 am, then 2:00, then 3:00, then 4:00 am, I decided that I would not stay there any longer.

When I was arrested, my whole world crumbled. I knew that leaders of political parties had been arrested and never heard from again. My only chance at survival was to find a way to escape from the jail. I was thinking about my cousin Józef Otto Rogatty, two years younger than me, who had escaped prison the previous year. He had been studying at the missionary seminary in Nónin at the start of the war when he was promptly taken as a prisoner of war by the Nazis. After multiple unsuccessful attempts, he finally escaped on January 14, 1945, and became a priest a few years later.

The room I was in was on the ground floor. When I looked out the window, I noticed that the surrounding buildings were three stories high and built together in a square. I noticed that, when the guard left periodically, he was usually gone for about ten to fifteen minutes. That would be my chance to escape.

I opened the window where there was no bar blocking it, and this surprised me. I jumped out the window, down to the ground. I noticed that there was a courtyard, but from both sides, there was a square building with no way to get out! I looked up to get an idea, and could not believe that nobody was shooting at me. I expected that the Secret Soviet Police would start shooting at me, but nothing happened. The walls were flat with nothing to hold on to. I looked around and saw a gutter for me to climb along the pipeline to the roof. The gutters were on an overhang, and it seemed impossible to get over the edge, but somehow, I found something on the roof steady enough to hold on to that allowed me to swing myself up onto it. It was very difficult to make it up to the roof, but I was pretty strong and young.

Once on the roof, I had to figure out how to get down. I decided that it was worth the risk to climb down the street side of the building by holding on to the gutters. From one roof, I jumped to a lower roof to the ground. Somehow, I survived and was able to leave the area without being discovered.

I knew that I did not have much time to see my wife Jadwiga, because our home would soon be under observation for sure. Jadwiga had just found out she was pregnant with our first child. She gave me a loaf of bread and money and told me I must disappear. I still have a piece of this bread today! It is hard as a rock, but I kept it all these years.

Jadwiga had been in the hair salon when I had been captured. She saw me walking in the company of the two soldiers, so she had some warning that nothing good was about to happen. She gave me the address of her parents in Warsaw. After stopping by a friend's house to get additional money and clothing in order to be able to leave the country quickly, I headed for the railroad station. But then I decided that I wouldn't be able to buy a ticket in Derlow because the Soviet Secret Police probably notified the local railroad station. So I walked along the tracks to the next town. I had a plan to go to the president of the county capital of our Polish Peasant party. He gave me shelter and sent his daughter to the station to buy a ticket for Warsaw. She came back with the ticket and gave it to me. I went back to the station but did not enter in the normal way. I let the train pass and jumped on it from the other side where nobody would see me enter and traveled to Warsaw.

When I had been held in the Soviet jail, the soldier had taken away from me all of my documents and money. Because I had been arrested, I had no document to use to identify myself. I was really in trouble. Everywhere in September 1946, they were looking for young people my age who were supposed to be registered in the military district office for a draft. Everyone who registered received a yellow piece of paper as evidence of registration. That meant you would be drafted at some time in the future. Young people were stopped all the time and asked to show the yellow paper; then they would be allowed to go free. But I no longer had this paper since the police took it from me, so when I was on the train to Warsaw, I was worrying that a military patrol would enter my compartment and ask for the yellow piece of paper. Then it would show on my face that I was nervous.

Sitting on the train in terrible fear of being discovered without identification, I happened to notice that someone in my train compartment was reading a newspaper and looking at me from time to time. For some unknown reason, he walked right up to me and quietly handed me a yellow piece of identification paper. He told me, "Memorize this name and place and date of birth." Then he left the compartment.

I looked at the yellow paper, memorized the information, and thought to myself, *What just happened?* I followed his instructions and put the yellow paper in my pocket. Imagine that in about fifteen minutes, a military patrol entered my compartment and asked for me to show my yellow piece of paper! I presented it, he looked at it, and I was safe. I couldn't figure out who that person was who gave me that paper. Later on, I was thinking about it and decided it must have been someone from the Polish underground, helping people trying to avoid service in the Soviet-occupying army. I was lucky that I met such a guardian angel!

While on the train, I was thinking about how quickly my life had changed. I had married Jadwiga on September 18, 1946, and we were living a wonderful life together. Then on December 7, I was arrested. When the train arrived in Warsaw, I went to my wife's parents' home. When I arrived there and knocked on the door, my mother-in-law fainted at the sight of me! Her husband helped her.

I said, "What happened?"

He answered, "Just a few minutes ago, there were members of the Soviet Secret Police here asking for you. She was so overwhelmed that she fainted." The Soviet Secret Police had searched the home. To my great surprise and disgust, they had taken a jar containing my appendix!

I had always believed that it was important to have all of my body parts with me when I died. My appendix had been removed during the war, without any anesthesia. It seems strange now, but I kept my appendix in preservative in a jar. When the Soviet Secret Police were searching the house and demanded alcohol from my in-laws, they could not stop the man from drinking from the jar with my appendix!

In any case, it was clear that I could not stay there. I went to my wife's uncle's home in a suburb of Warsaw. He gave me shelter, and I had a little time to think about my situation. It was there that I learned that all the other members of my party's leadership in Derlow had been arrested, just as I was. But they were not so fortunate as to escape.

I kept thinking about how I was unjustly arrested. I had had the best intentions. I was a teacher of junior college, and I could not figure out why this was so offensive to the Communist Party that they felt it was necessary to stop me from doing this. I was active in political circles. The prime minister of Poland's government-in-exile in London during the war, Stanisław Mikołajczyk, returned to Poland in 1946 to become deputy premier and re-build his political party, to which most Poles belonged: Polskie Stronnictwo Ludowe which was the Polish Peasant Party. This party was traditional, democratic, and against the Communist Party. The goal was to keep Poland as Poland, a free Poland without any connections to the Soviet Union. Now that Mikołajczyk was back in Poland, the Polish people felt it was time to have an election and see who was in favor of keeping Poland independent. Stalin had agreed with Churchill and Roosevelt that Poland was supposed to have an elected government.

I decided to go to meet with government officials to challenge my arrest. I was naïve, but at that time, I felt it was my duty to try to show the local powers of the Communist party that Poland still had a democratic system in the western sense. I went to the national council government organization that was a substitute of a Parliament because it was before elections to Parliament. I went to the legal advisor to the national council and explained to him that I was a member of the local municipal council in Derlow. After listening to my story, he told me I should go abroad. He tried to persuade me that one person was unable to oppose the powers of the Communists, so he advised me that this would be the only way for me to survive.

I still did not believe that leaving the country was the right thing to do, so I went to the office of the Polish Peasant Party where Stanisław Mikołajczyk, the prime minister, was the leader. He was at a conference, but his second-in-command, Stefan Korboński, received me.

I asked him, "What should I do? I was arrested on December 7, 1946. My people in Derlow told me that I was supposed to be the Peasant Party candidate in January 1947. When I was supposed to have a campaign meeting, I was always denied. Where's the freedom? What's going on?"

He said, "Everything's fine with the party here in Warsaw. Things are going so well here that we now even have our own newspaper."

I told him, "In the capital, you are treated like a legitimate political party, but in the provinces, we are thrown in jail. What protection do you have? I thought you would have power to help me?"

He answered, "Yes, we have this power. There must be some kind of misunderstanding."

I said, "The rest of the members of my party's leadership in Derlow were all arrested. I was the lucky one—the only one who escaped. The rest were not lucky. They are all still in jail."

He told me, "Go see the prosecutor in Derlow and tell him that you saw me, and he will let you go because it's of course illegal to arrest you."

But I told him, "I will *not* return there. I know that they will not listen. They don't know you or the prime minister and disregard the existence of our party because they are Communists. They have started a dictatorship of Communism. You here in Warsaw don't feel it. But in the provinces, it's destructive."

Korboński said, "Change your name and go to some other area like Siberia or Eastern Poland."

I said, "I am a married man, my wife is expecting a baby, and I cannot do such a thing. I lived like a rabbit during the German occupation for five-and-a-half years, and I do not want to do that again. I am in Poland, and I want Poland to be governed by a Polish democratic government."

He said, "We want this too, but the road is long to achieve it. How about you join guerilla warfare?"

I said, "I've had enough of that during the German occupation. Do you expect me to shoot other Poles just because they are red and I am not red? No, I don't want to repeat what happened in Spain where Spanish were killing each other."

After talking with him some more, he eventually told me that the only thing to do to survive is simply leave the country. There was no other way.

After receiving this disappointing news, I had to see Jadwiga. I could not go to her parents' home since the Secret Police had looked for me there. Instead, I went to her uncle's home in Warsaw, where she later joined me. We tried to take our minds off our desperate situation by going to the theater. The show was called *The Devil's Disciple*.

After that, we boarded a train to the Czechoslovakia border. It was so hard to leave my pregnant wife, but Jadwiga told me that it was our only option. I promised to come back and get her as soon as I could.

After Czechoslovakia, I went to Hamburg, Germany, occupied by America and Britain, then Denmark, before arriving in Sweden. When I got to Czechoslovakia, I stayed with a family; the wife was Polish, and the husband was Czech. But, at that time, the Communists were already demonstrating and making all kinds of noise there, so I could not stay long. I left for Germany. In Hamburg, I visited a refugee camp of former Polish soldiers who had fought on the British side, and I got sick with a terrible flu while in a hotel in Hamburg. Somebody told me that there was a Polish military hospital, so I went there and got help from the Polish doctors. When I recovered, I went to Denmark, but I could not stay because the government was trading with Communist Poland. They told me that the Danish government would send me back to Poland if I stayed in Denmark. Some people told me that Sweden would take refugees and help them to immigrate wherever they wanted without sending them back to their home country.

I arrived in Sweden and registered with the police, who informed the State Department. They gave me permission to stay as a political refugee in Stockholm. Then someone from the employment office in Stockholm came to interview me. This was about the time that the Polish elections were taking place in January 1947, and the Swedish were interested in hearing the truth from me firsthand, rather than reading about it from a Polish journalist. The U.S. was also interested in hearing about my experience in Poland. In fact, I was told that I had a visa waiting for me to the U.S. and that it would expire soon because they wanted me to come right away to the U.S. as a political refugee and tell them about what was going on in Poland. But I never used that visa, because I couldn't leave my wife with an entire ocean between us. I would have to wait a few more years to get another U.S. visa once I had my wife with me, but it was worth it. I also declined any interview from Swedish or U.S. reporters because of my concerns over my "stateless" status.

The man from the Swedish foreign ministry interviewing me was very nice and friendly. I spoke with him in German because I did not know how to speak Swedish yet. First we tried French, but he said he was better at speaking German, and I knew German very well by this time. This was a very important person, close to a deputy level. He made notes of my story, and why I had to leave the country. He said he would help me get my wife with me once I got settled in Sweden and learned the language. I later learned that this kind man kept his promises.

When I was talking with him, I asked what my future would be. He told me, "Get a job, and simply try to forget what happened in Poland and adjust to a new life."

When I got my first job near Stockholm in Tullinge in the iron foundry of the Alfa-Laval Separator factory, it was like I imagined hell to be—very hot, dangerous, and noisy. It was unhealthy because of the exposure to constant smoke and vapors. It was hard labor. I developed strong muscles like a wrestler.

The Soviet Secret Police intercepted many of the letters I wrote to Jadwiga from Sweden to Poland. But here are a couple I wrote to Jadwiga that she received while I was working in Tullinge. She was still pregnant at the time, but our son, Marek, died three days after his birth in August 1947.

Stockholm 14 Feb 1947

My dearest wife!

My sweet Jadzia, I won't beat about the bush. My work is very hard. I work at an iron foundry. Smoke, dust, just dark. I prepare sand for molds and need to move the sand from one place to the other, onto a large sieve, pour water over it and constantly mix. Then I need to lift and carry heavy iron casts. It is very dark from the dust. I can hardly see anything. The supervisors won't let us have a rest for a moment. How long will we take this? I am an intellectual, not like the supervisor and the rest. I am not bothered. I need to do my work. The Polish workers are very good people. They give good advice and help one another. They are all ex-prisoners of war, so they know what misery is.

Love, Tad

Tullinge 2 March 1947

My sweet little child! My gold Jadzinek!

I am still at damn Tullinge. It is the last day anyway. Tomorrow morning I'm leaving. I have just written a card to your cousin in Belgium. The rascal is not replying. And my cousins from the USA are not replying either. I don't know what it means. Maybe they don't want to know me? Anything goes. Do you love me? Tomorrow I am going to an unknown direction. I have been traveling to so many unknown places that it even doesn't bother me anymore. Why am I going there? First of all, I want to earn lots of money, and I have heard they pay well there. Secondly, I want to speak Swedish as soon as possible, and the work there is supposed to be lighter (as I was assured at the employment agency), so I will have more time, because I won't be so tired as here after work. I will also have my own room—that's another plus. After some time, I will return nearer Stockholm, so I am closer to the consulate offices. Most probably to Uppsala where I could be just now but don't want to be just yet as the work isn't that great and it is badly paid. For the time I am going to be at that slaughterhouse where I am going to start working. The agency is looking for a better job for me in Stockholm.

Here in Sweden, the possibilities of a permanent stay are rather slim. You need to wait about 10 years to get a citizenship and for all this time you are a foreigner that no one in Sweden cares much about. Here they need loads of men to work but not like me. One of the Polish people said: "Here they need strong and stupid people." It is true in a way. There are a lot of intelligent people here and not many to work. There are lots of work ads that they also need white collar workers, but a foreigner won't get this type of work. I know one thing for sure: I will not be a physical worker for the rest of my life. Once I master the language, I'll be fine. Perhaps then even as a foreigner, I will get a job as a sales correspondent in a company. I am also learning English. When I master this language as well, we'll be just fine. In the meantime, I need to stick with what I have. I am hoping to earn quite a bit in the summer digging up turf. Until then, I need to be with you. What do you think?

If we don't manage to get to the USA, I am hoping to go to Canada, South Africa, or South America. I can live anywhere. That is with you, of course. In South Africa, the Polish people who went there made such big amounts of fortune on trade that they don't need to work until the rest of their lives. And that's within 2 years. Why wouldn't we manage? You can always return to Poland anyway. I think that with masses of dollars, they would greet us even in a nicer way rather than poor and ragged like we are now. What do you think? Just learn English. You are good at trading, and I am not too bad either. In the meantime, try and find some possibilities of travel.

Here when you have about 200 crowns, you can travel even to the end of the world. Everyone will have you. I am not going to buy anything for myself here. I am going to open a savings account, and every month I am going to put some money towards savings. And you, Jadzik, try everything you can to join me. You are my wife and, as such, have every right to visit me. It is not only a human right but according to the international refugee law. A husband has every right to import his wife. I can't do it at the moment, as I am still looking for work that will provide for you and me. In the application, I need to state that I am able to provide for you as my income is so and so.

However, currently it is nothing. When that's sorted, then I will not rest (and so won't you) until I have you with me. The application needs to be written in Swedish, so it requires some time from me to be able to speak and write all by myself. But don't you worry. I've heard of someone who brought their mother within 2.5 months. So why can't I have my wife here? I have a greater right for this.

But don't lose your spirit. Think positively. Don't worry because our little one needs to be brave and manly. God forbid he can't be short-tempered or pampered. We need to bring him up to be a good man. If you love me, from now on you're going to be brave. You won't break down, will you? You need to write this to me. Remember that you have a husband and you belong with him. The state acknowledged this relationship, so the state cannot break this relationship in any way. The state needs to help you to join your husband if you are not going to be a burden to the state. Of course, the next thing that I need is to provide for you and the baby. I want to fulfill my obligation. If I am forced to be here and now, it is just because of the stupidity of irresponsible factors. Am I a criminal? If they are going to get rid of people from Poland like me, then who will stay there anyway? If only I knew for what and why. I am here because of some people of unsound mind's stupid whim. Nevertheless, I am not wasting my time here, and I am trying to fulfill my duty as a husband and future father.

Love, Tad

One day while I was at work at Separator, some co-workers in the restroom asked me about where I was from. I was naïve to think that it was all right to tell them my life story. I thought I had done the right thing by opposing Communism. But these Swedish co-workers were members of the Communist party! My wife was later very upset with me when she found out that I told these co-workers about myself. After they listened to me for a while, they said, "You are not one of us; you are against us."

I told the workers, "So what? You should be better educated about the situation. Don't you know that Communists want to take over the entire world?"

The workers said, "We are enemies of capitalism, and you are one of them; so what are you doing here, spying on us?" My co-workers no longer wanted to talk with me, and we went back to work.

A day or two later, when the iron was melting in big containers, an operator was moving them. When each container would come to where I was standing, I would prepare forms, and then it would pour the iron into the forms. Those workers like me who were preparing the forms were standing and watching how well the iron was filling the forms. When the iron was formed, there would be a terrible smell with smoke and vapors.

Well, suddenly, someone pushed me on a heap of soil and said, "Run, right away from here!" I got up and left to the restroom, and at that moment when I was away from my forms, the container overturned and spread a lot of iron all over.

The worker who had warned me followed me to the restroom and said, "Disappear from this place right away. Not only from Stockholm, but go to a province far away, because what just happened was revenge from the Communists who you told your story. You're supposed to be dead. I'm a refugee from Estonia, but I keep my mouth shut. You should also do this. Don't talk about those things."

And I left right away and did not even go to the office. I wish I could say that I learned from my mistake, but a couple of years later,

I found myself in a similar predicament in my first job working in New York.

After this attempt on my life in Stockholm in 1947, I took a train far away and got a job in Stenstorp, Sweden. I became a hog catcher at a slaughterhouse called Skaraborgs Läns Slakteriförening. I had to transfer hogs from trucks to a holding pen and then to the butchery.

7 March 47

My beloved wife! I have just received a letter from my brother. He usually only talks about women fairly generally, but he admires you wholeheartedly. He says that "you are an ideal wife" or "an ideal of resourcefulness and entrepreneurship, etc. etc. She is absolutely fine. In the meantime, you need to be satisfied with this enumeration of her virtues." Have you noticed that he is discretely not interfering in our marriage life? Not even a word about this. That's what I like about him.

Tomorrow it will have been five days since I started my job in Stenstorp. I have never thought that in my life I would be a hog catcher. In my work life, I have done many things, but I have never done this, and I have never dreamed about this "privilege." The most important thing is that the laborers from here are very decent toward me. Can you imagine me as a hog catcher? Don't be embarrassed that your husband is currently doing this job. It will be different soon. Man needs to experience many things in his life. Good things and bad things. The work is not hard at all but terribly stinky and very dangerous because you can catch some nasty sickness. I will try and quit this job soon. Sometimes life brings you these things. It is all really nothing; it will pass. It is worse for laborers who realize very well that they will do the same job for the rest of their lives.

I am going to have my dinner soon. I don't know if I have told you, but the Swedish people really enjoy eating horse meat. Same in Denmark. I also eat it. I even do not realize that I am eating it when it is served to me. Do you love me? If you do, then you will write to me now a good and loving letter. Jadzia, my dearest wife, be patient and wait. I am going to have my supper now. Tell me, "enjoy your meal!" It is nearly 7:00 in the evening. Surely you must be eating your dinner now with your parents.

I have laid out all the photos of you on the table. I am wearing my glasses because I don't want to miss anything. I am looking and looking at you, and I can't get enough. You are so pretty but also very far away. I miss you so much. You give me strength. Do you think it is pleasant to work among some total boors, especially when it is physically exhausting? The native laborers don't know what a war is—they are very limited. There is one Estonian with whom I communicate in Russian. It if was not for him, I would not be able to speak with anyone. Well, perhaps that is a bit of an exaggeration because I have picked up some Swedish and so it is not too bad. Goodbye, my dear. Kisses for you and on your tummy. I send my love to your parents.

Your loving husband, Tad

Here is one of the letters Jadwiga wrote to me at this time in my life.

Włochy, 7 March 47

My beloved Tadzik! My dear husband!

I have received your postcard of 25.02.47. My cousin came to the conclusion that there is no point wandering and working as a farmhand somewhere in foreign lands. Every Pole abroad is taken advantage of in a defiant way. He is used for the worst and the toughest jobs; a native is always first. The conclusion is that you need to work hard everywhere for your piece of brown or white bread; it doesn't matter. People have their worries, financial problems everywhere, literally everywhere. Everywhere is better where we are not—that's how the saying goes. A Pole is best off in Poland. That's the conclusion. Listen, I am having some ideas about America. Are you still thinking of doing silly things like in Derłowo? You were holding on to a few things, but eventually, nothing worked out. Is it going to be the same way this time? I have no way of stopping you doing many ridiculous things. Your responsibility is to make plans for me to see you and not to travel any further. Calm down, and don't be led by some pretty words.

I am waiting for your letters. Tadzik, we have little time to think about whether you can use the right to amnesty. Tell me what you think about it, straight away. If you decide to return, write to me in the first place. Can you really expect me to live off my parents for years? It can't be this way. You need to make an immediate decision. If there is a decision for me to join you, then everything is changing its perspective. You need to think about the responsibilities you have, and that you are not on your own, you have your wife. My darling, believe me, your letters brighten up my grey life. However, sometimes I feel a bit rebellious. You know when it started—from that letter you wrote to Mr. Olusiński about going to Africa. I had no idea about your plans and to learn that somebody knew before me—that's despicable. Are we going back to the times with your old girlfriend Krystyna? Sometimes by saying a few silly sentences, you can hurt someone right in their heart. I don't want any frictions between us because they are not making us any closer to each other; quite the opposite, they keep you apart from each other. I am waiting for a letter from you. I am not going to write anymore because it is getting late. Good night kisses, my kitty.

Love, Jadwiga

Jadwiga Haska, Warsaw, Poland 1946; Written on back of photo:
"Remember that somewhere far away there is a heart that beats only for you
and waits for you with great longing.—Jadwiga"

My job at the slaughterhouse was a job no one else wanted, but it was one of the only jobs I was able to get as an immigrant and refugee. It was a crematorium of animals that died on farms of disease. According to Swedish law, such animals could not be disposed of by farmers; they had to be sent to a slaughterhouse to be inspected by a veterinarian so that the government would know what diseases plagued farm animals in the country. After inspection, animal corpses were cooked or burned, and the fat was separated to make margarine. The meat was made into flour that was sent back to farms as food for animals. The bones were ground into flour used as fertilizer.

The veterinarian and part-owner of the slaughterhouse was a kind man named Dr. Herbert Malmsten. I still keep in touch with all of his children to this day. Dr. Malmsten came to where I was working, engaged me in conversation, invited me to his home for dinner, and asked me to tell my story. I could not believe that this man was inviting me, a foreigner and low-level worker, to his home. I met his lovely wife Disa and their children Göran, Bengt, Birgitta, and Nisse. I would read the kids stories in Swedish, and they would help correct my pronunciation.

Dr. Malmsten said that I had been right to leave Stockholm so quickly without telling anyone where I was going. I said, "Why do you have Communists in such a paradise as Sweden?"

He said that in Sweden you have the extreme left (the Communists) and the right. He told me that by talking to Communists, I had exposed myself to danger, and he said he was willing to help me any way he could. I told him my wife was still in Poland; I could not take her with me because I barely was able to escape myself. She was pregnant; how could I expose a pregnant wife to travel to the unknown? Of course, I wanted to reunite with her, but could not do so under those circumstances. My only crime was that I was so young and naïve to believe that if more people were thinking like me, then we would be the majority and we would not let Communists take over by voting for a democratic government instead of a Communist government. My father-in-law shared my view, and it got him into trouble throughout his life as well. That's probably why Jadwiga always warned me that it was best not to tell others about my beliefs. She was very upset with me for running for political office.

I wrote to the Polish government multiple times to try to persuade them to allow me to return to Poland legally and join my wife. I filed a complaint against the commandant Zdzislaw Kowalski for wrongfully arresting me. Below is the letter I wrote to the district prosecutor in Slupsk after my complaint was not acknowledged:

> *I would like to ask you once again to investigate in detail how I deserved to be imprisoned on December 7, 1946. As a Polish citizen, the constitution gives me the right to seek clarification on the matter by the state prosecutor. Before leaving the country, I did not go to the prosecutor's office because I was afraid that I would have to sit innocently in jail pending trial, and that would last months. I preferred not to take this risk because every restriction of liberty causes me a nervous breakdown (a "souvenir" from occupation times due to my fear of the Gestapo). I think that you cannot expel people who want to stay in Poland and work for the country. It would be contrary to the order of President Bolesław Bierut, who calls all Poles to return to the country.*
>
> *All the more tragic, because I am entirely innocent. From a socio-political point of view, I should not be treated as a representative of the bourgeoisie. I am the son of a six-acre Pomeranian peasant. I lost my father at the age of eleven, mother at thirteen, and I had to survive without any help from the state or from relatives, gaining an education through my*

own hard work. I did not know a carefree childhood or happy years of youth; I only knew hunger and cold. I fought for a piece of bread and to attend university.

To be a good citizen, do I have to be like Galician revolutionist Jakub Szela and have on my conscience blood of my brother Poles, who have already decimated the German invasion? If the Prosecutor is silent and cannot answer why I was arrested, maybe this "crime" is not yet in the Polish code? Because I was "ill-thinking" and did not agree with the Communists. Until now, the world's codices have been silent when it came to crimes committed in thought. Only religion knows such sins. I regret that the Polish State does not know the means to punish the murderers of the deputy minister of national defense, and, instead, punishes a man who, by his deeds, proved that he thinks and works for the good of the country. The Swedes have a proverb, "Small thieves hang, and the biggest criminals are released." The word "thief" is used figuratively here. Once again, please send me the official decision of the Prosecutor of the Republic of Poland regarding my imprisonment. At the same time, I am asking for the return of personal documents taken from me.

The only response I received was that the commandant who arrested me was cleared of any wrongdoing due to insufficient proof. At this point, I decided I should focus my attention on smuggling my wife from Poland to Sweden and learning the English language in the hopes that we could someday emigrate to the U.S. and have the opportunity for a better life.

I knew a lot of languages (eight at the time), but English was much more difficult. To improve my English language skills, I ordered a Linguaphone course from Stockholm and they sent me a set of records and a manual. I bought a Gramophone to listen to the records and start studying English. But first when I listened, it sounded like garbled sounds that were impossible to understand. I wrote a letter to Linguaphone, sending the records back, and requested a course for beginners, not advanced English learners.

But they responded by saying that this was indeed a course for beginners. They advised me to listen not just once or twice, but hundreds of times to each record; only then would I understand and have a feel for the language. I was determined to learn this language. So I took a piece of paper and a pencil and every time I listened once, I made a mark, and then another mark, another mark, four marks, five, and when I had twenty-five marks, it was one hundred times, and when I opened up the textbook, I could follow each word, even though I could not understand it. I learned that "beautiful" was pronounced "beautiful," and not "be—a—oo—tee—full." After I completed fifty lessons, I learned the basics of English pretty well, even with correct pronunciation. And then I learned how to listen without wasting time.

At the time I took this course, when I was cooking, washing, cleaning, or eating, I was listening and marking the paper. I was exposed to English for quite some time by listening to each lesson a hundred times. So later on, when I was going through announcements for U.S. jobs, it was not too difficult to respond to them. I wrote to the linguistics company, thanking them for their advice, and told them that they were right when they insisted on multiple listenings, not just once or twice. And I also told them that, for the first lesson, it was necessary for me to listen one hundred times, but by the fiftieth lesson, I only needed to listen five times to master it.

CHAPTER 4

Smuggling My Wife
Out of Poland

Now that I had saved some money and learned Swedish and some English, it was time to focus on getting my wife back with me. Dr. Malmsten supported me in my plans to get my Jadwiga to Sweden. He took out his checkbook and said I should offer money to someone to smuggle my wife to Sweden. He signed a blank check and instructed me to use however much money I needed. He was a very generous man, but I did not want to accept this check because I did not know if I'd be able to use it. But he convinced me to take it and instructed me to take leave from work and go to some bars in Stockholm where I could meet Swedish sailors. He said there would be plenty of them willing to do this job for me.

After I interviewed many of these sailors, I quickly became aware of the fact that they were not reliable. They were drunks. I went to an office for sailors and tried to recruit those who were not drunk. I tried to persuade them. Some said, "Yes, of course," but I could not trust them, and others said, "No, I do not want to take the risk." I also was worried about the risk. I was concerned about risking money that was not mine.

Then I went to a Polish organization in Stockholm that helped refugees. These beautiful people advised me not to trust the drunk sailors because they didn't have a conscience and would betray my wife. I decided that if I could not safely bribe a sailor, then I would have to become a Swedish sailor myself in order to smuggle my wife to Sweden. I started by completing all the necessary paperwork so that once she was in Sweden, she could be there legally.

Getting myself a Swedish passport was not easy. I had to go to Skara, a small city, at least two hours from Stenstorp, to apply for a passport at the police station. The Chief of Police arrogantly told me that a refugee does not have the opportunity to get a Swedish passport. He said, "Impossible! You should know better. You could be a spy taking photographs of our harbors, and then sell this information to the Soviets. If you want to be eligible to apply for citizenship, you need to live here at least ten years."

I asked to use the telephone and made a long-distance call through an operator to the foreign ministry officer who had promised to help me when I first arrived in Sweden. I still had his business card in my wallet. When the officer came on the phone, I reminded him of meeting me nine months ago, and to my relief, he remembered me. He asked for the police chief to be put on the phone. When the police chief heard to whom he was talking, he jumped out of the chair, stood in attention, took careful notice, and responded to his orders, "Yes, sir."

I happily left the police station with a Swedish passport and all the required stamps and signatures. Now I could try to become a Swedish sailor.

When I arrived at the harbormaster's office to apply to become a sailor, I was once again told that this could not be done. I called the foreign ministry official in Stockholm, told him what I wanted, and he asked me to put the harbormaster on the phone. When they got off the phone, the harbormaster informed me that I would get my wish of becoming a sailor and getting my wife to Sweden.

He gave me a Swedish sailor identification book, and cleverly helped me get around the rules. Where it asked for my country of birth, instead of writing "Poland," he printed that I was "registered in the Swedish church books." Anyone who is born in Sweden appears in the church books. So this wasn't a lie, but a bit evasive.

Now that I had both a Swedish passport, and a Swedish sailor identification book, I could even go to Poland if I was stopped. I traveled as a Swedish sailor to Poland three times before developing the perfect plan to smuggle my wife with me back to Sweden.

Tadeusz Haska working as a sailor in Sweden on the ship Kisa
so that he could smuggle his wife out of Poland, 1947.

My plan was complete just in time, because Jadwiga had been losing faith in me, and she later told me that her parents told her to forget about me because I would not come back for her.

Włochy 12 March 1947

My dear Tadzik!

*My gem! I could not sleep all night, this is how much
I was worried about your letters. I don't want you to be
some kind of a farm-hand abroad with no rights. Why
are you working so much, for who and what for? You
are not going to make any fortunes there. The pay is
poor, from what you are writing. They are despicable.
I hate them. They are tormenting you and using your
energy. I feel nothing but repulsion for them. As for
your return—God forbid I am not imposing anything,
do as you please, just like two months ago. I am led by
my reason like any wife or mother. I need to be your
mother in a way, you lost yours so early. Your mom,
if she was alive, surely would like you to return and
not to wander among strangers. I would like you very
much to bring about 50 or 30 kronor, and of course only
if you can manage. If all fails, I think my departure
from this country will be a great tragedy. You won't
be able to return, and I won't be able to return either.
Anyway, there is really nothing to talk about, there is
no future for you, you are not going to be a laborer.
Come back, you'll be studying and working, I will also
help you, with some God's will we will survive. It is
important that we love each other. God will give us
his blessings. If you don't want to come back, send me
your reply by a telegram: "I am not coming back," and
if you do, say: "I am coming back." Our fate hangs in
the air. It is no good for you over there. I know you
are suffering morally and spiritually. All these years
of your studying will go to waste. Here when you get*

your diploma, we will also make our way somewhere
but together. It is a waste of an academic year for you.
If you come back, perhaps you will be able to catch
up with your studies. Consider everything and write
to me straight away. I am waiting for a wise solution
to this issue and taking my opinion into account. The
conditions you have there you will have over here.
Perhaps your life will be a bit worse. However, your job
will be easier. I send you countless kisses on your lips.

Yours forever,
Jadzinek

PS. Kisses from my parents and granny. My mom
says you should come back.

On top of this loss of faith in me, Jadwiga suffered the death of
our son, Marek, three days after his birth. I felt terrible that she did
not have access to adequate medical care due to my fugitive status.
She had seen a doctor during her pregnancy who had advised her
that the baby would need to be delivered by c-section. But when she
went into labor, the doctor on duty had just graduated from medical
school that same year and believed that he could deliver the baby in
the natural way. He used forceps, causing severe damage to our son's
brain. Our son only lived three days after that. The loss of our first
child was devastating to us, and even more so because we were not
together when it happened.

Włochy, 15 August 1947

My dearest Tadzik!

Today is the Assumption of Mary celebration. I need to say that I miss you more and more with every day. I don't know if you approve of what I have done. So, I gave our baby's things to a very poor woman who can't buy these things. As a "symbol," I kept one bib. These things were driving me crazy anyway. I am trying to forget, but it is so hard. I am terribly worried about you; do you understand me? Be wise with whatever you're doing. Currently, I live in a terrible tension. There is always something new in every letter. So, I await the letters with great anxiety. It is better for me if I stayed at my uncle's. Firstly, it is because I cannot lift heavy things and to "S" you cannot get any porters. Currently, I feel very lonely, more than ever before. You can get crazy from all of this.

Love, J.

Just as she was about to give up on me, Jadwiga went to Częstochowa in a last effort to pray for my return. The Black Virgin of Częstochowa is a miracle place in Poland where a painting of the Virgin hangs in the church. The very next day after praying there, she received a letter from me telling her I was coming to get her! Jadwiga carried the picture below of the Black Virgin in her pocketbook every day for the rest of her life. Everyone who came to our home would also see a copy of the picture hanging on the wall.

The Black Madonna of Częstochowa is an icon of the Virgin Mary housed at the Jasna Góra Monastery in Częstochowa, Poland, where Jadwiga Haska prayed for Tadeusz's return.

8 September 1947

Dear Tad,

My mother brought me 5 letters today and one card from you. What a joy! Today I am feeling well. The doctor made a joke that I was nearly on the gravedigger's spade but managed to escape! Hopefully, I will be discharged on Monday. I am very happy about it. From what I can see, you have been terribly affected by our misfortune the same as me. Don't worry about my health. I have made a full recovery now. My darling, you know I had lost all hope and perhaps I said something unfinished when I talked about our baby's death. For all the letters I received from you now I love you even more! You gave your proof of love. As you can see, the minute

I feel better, I write letters to my lovely husband! I know your plan; there is no need for any details. Whenever I think about seeing you, I instantly feel well. I am ready to go there even tomorrow. Nothing will stand in our way. Tadeusz, hurry up and just do it. I feel so terrible without you. I love you very much and kiss you a million times.

Your Jadzinek

I wrote Jadwiga the letter about my plans to smuggle her in Polish using secret code words so that it would not be understood by authorities censoring it. The plan was for her to meet me at the Baltic coast. She later told me that her mother was crying with worry that she would never see her daughter again. Jadwiga was happy that I was coming for her but had to deal with a lot of fear and harassment while waiting for me to come. The day before I came for her, she and her mother were out for a walk and ran into the woman who had cleaned their home before the war. The woman greeted them and said that her daughter married a police officer, and wanted to get together with Jadwiga. She was so nervous about being around a police officer that she made up some excuse about why she could not visit the woman. Jadwiga's mother was always worried someone was following her. They were always unsure of whether a policeman was the real police or the "secret" police.

Jadwiga had a great fear of the Soviets because she remembered when they took over her home city of Warsaw in January 1945. When she was out walking with her mother during that time, a Russian soldier demanded that she give him the gold ring on her finger, a precious gift from her father. The soldier threatened to cut off her finger if she refused, so her mother gave him the ring, and Jadwiga was heartbroken.

When Jadwiga went to try to find me in jail after my arrest the previous year, she noticed that the police chief had taken my beautiful watch and wallet. When she asked him where I was, the police were very rude to her and refused to tell her. They told her, "If we see him on the street, we will shoot him like an animal."

Jadwiga could not believe that this was happening in her beloved Poland. The secretary of the Communist party kept coming to her asking where I was. He told her that his sister is a nurse who told him about our family. He told Jadwiga, "If I did not know your mother is from the Borzym family, then you would not be here right now."

Jadwiga never took threats well. She asked him, "Do you see this tree? There will come a time when I will come to this tree right here and find you hanging from it." The Communist leader repeated his threat a second time, as did Jadwiga, who ended the conversation: "If I will not hang you from the tree, then somebody else will do it. Goodbye." My brave wife was twenty-two years old at the time!

The time to smuggle Jadwiga out of Poland had finally arrived. She later told me that she was shocked to see such a "shabby looking" man at her motel door. The shabby man was my sailor friend who happened to be the second-in-command of the ship that would take us out of Poland. He advised her to walk around to get acquainted with the area from where they would be leaving Poland in the morning but warned her that on the right side of the area was a naval base where 4,000 Soviet soldiers were stationed. He instructed her to buy some good alcohol because he would need it to pay someone for his help. The sailor told her that he would come back for her in the morning. She told him that it would be better to leave that same night because the boat may decide to leave early. That's exactly what happened, so it was good that Jadwiga insisted on leaving at night.

When I arrived, her mother was dying with fear, standing there crying. I was very drunk, but it was on purpose so that I would look like the other sailors. Jadwiga did not know that I was going to show up drunk, so this was very upsetting to her.

As we made our way toward the port where the ship carrying coal was docked, my sailor friend instructed Jadwiga and me that we could not go the official way using the boardwalk, because there were always policemen checking identification papers of those coming and going. Instead, he led us across a bridge that had been destroyed by war activities—either German or Soviet. Then we walked through a territory of Soviet sailors. We had to walk through a quay without being stopped by the Soviets. My sailor friend and I had deliberately gotten drunk so that the Soviets would not stop us. If we had not been drunk, they would have assumed that we were spies and would try to stop us. My sailor friend made sure that we had a bottle of alcohol to give to any Soviets that tried to stop us.

We were about to approach the most terrifying part of our journey to the ship. The territory between the river and the quay was full of four kilometers of mines that the Germans didn't bother to remove after the war. There was no other way to get to the ship without being noticed.

My sailor friend promised to get us through the minefield. He said, "If I happen to step on a mine, then you just follow over where I was killed, and you will have a route free of mines to the ship."

I said, "How can you talk this way?"

He said, "I am a bachelor, and I don't care for life. You have a family."

I said, "My goodness."

I saw Jadwiga trembling with fear and began to wish that she had been drunk too. But she had refused to drink. I had never before in my life been drunk until that day. And it was a good thing because we were soon stopped by two Soviet soldiers saying, "Stop. Who is coming?"

This is where being drunk came in handy. My sailor friend and I looked drunk and mumbled something incomprehensible. As planned we gave them a bottle of vodka, and they said, "Go ahead wherever you like."

Luckily we made it to the boat without hitting any mines. When we arrived, my Swedish sailor friends tried to carry on the suitcase containing Jadwiga's fur coat and other belongings. But the customs officials confiscated it because it was considered smuggling. The officials asked the sailors why they were carrying a suitcase, but they said nothing and thankfully did not betray Jadwiga. Once on the boat, we put her in hiding in a coffin so small that it was like a cage. I would come over to the box and let her know I was there by whispering to her. Soon after we boarded, fourteen members of the Polish police came on board to check the ship, to see if it was free of contraband or refugees!

Of course, I was so nervous that I was perspiring! Lucky for us, the second-in-command invited them to sit down, poured them large glasses of vodka, and got them drunk. They indicated that they wanted to look around, but my friend said, "You can look later, drink first." After they were drunk, they forgot why they came. They left, and we were safe.

Once we were safely at sea, my sailor friends and I went to the coffin where Jadwiga was hiding and asked her if she wanted to go to the cafeteria with us. She sternly answered, "Over my dead body." She was terrified of being discovered because this was a boat for male sailors only. But after hours of no food or drink, Jadwiga agreed to come out briefly, only because I told her that we were now far away from Poland.

Our main concern was to keep the captain from discovering Jadwiga had been smuggled on the ship. My sailor friends stood in front of her, blocking the captain's view so that he and the Swedish woman cook would not see her as we made our way to my cabin on the other side of the ship. The captain wouldn't tolerate smuggling because he did not want to lose his license. He relied on the cook to tell him if anyone was smuggled and then he would call the Polish authorities to take them back to Poland. He also warned that the last time this happened, the sailor disappeared at sea without a trace. My friend the second-in-command on the ship cautioned Jadwiga that if she opened her mouth, she would end up overboard in the water.

I was so afraid that the woman in charge of cleaning the ship would find Jadwiga and send me to the Polish authorities. Poor Jadwiga had to just sit there and wait.

Jadwiga had been terrified throughout the entire journey, worrying about what might happen. After many hours of my poor wife not being able to use the bathroom, we arrived in Sweden. I asked the young, second-in-command sailor to take Jadwiga off the ship to make it look like she was with him. The captain would have noticed if Jadwiga left with me and would have questioned me because he knew I was Polish. We arrived late at night in Sweden, and of course, the sailors' girlfriends were waiting for them. Some of them were invited onboard to spend the night on the ship, so it looked normal for the second-in-command to be walking with Jadwiga.

Since her suitcase had been confiscated, Jadwiga told the sailor that she did not have any money to pay him for his trouble, but that he could hold onto her grandpa's ring until she had enough money to get it back from him. He kindly agreed. A few weeks later, the sailor returned Jadwiga's ring; we gave him the money for his troubles, and everything was fine. The sailor was a hero. Not because of the ring, but because of the minefield that he led us across to get to the port area in Poland.

Surely someone had been watching over us to get us to Sweden safely. We lived there for two and a half years from 1947 to 1949. I later learned that the prime minister of Poland, Mikołajczyk, and Korboński, his second-in-command who advised me to leave the country, had also escaped arrest and fled Poland the month after I smuggled Jadwiga out of Poland. My friends from the Polish Peasant Party had been worried about me. I wrote a letter to Amelia Łączyńska, who became a successful writer, letting her know that Jadwiga and I were safe, and I continued to write her every couple of years until her death at age 100 in 1993.

Tadeusz and Jadwiga, reunited, at their home in Lidköping, Sweden.

My wife had a hard time adjusting to life in Sweden. But she got a good job painting china at the Rörstrand china factory in Lidköping where I was a supervisor in the warehouse. Jadwiga had always been artistic. She enjoyed the poetry of Adam Mickiewicz and Maria Konopnicka and the opera *Tosca*. Her favorite book was *Lalka* by Boleslaw Prus.

Jadwiga disliked the fact that she was paid 33% less than men for doing the same job at Rörstrand, and she argued that the women did a better job. There was an efficiency expert in the organization who Jadwiga compared to Hitler. He would deduct from the painters' pay if he caught them not working. The boss kept making them produce more and gave the men the easy jobs. Jadwiga complained that the men were always laughing or smoking. One time I went to visit her at her job, and she spoke quickly to me in Polish. Her boss was worried about what she might be saying and asked me to translate it. I told him she said she wanted a raise.

The Rörstrand china studio where Jadwiga Haska worked from
1947-1949 in Lidköping, Sweden.

The other challenge for my poor Jadwiga was that nightmares
about our life in Poland plagued her. After I had been arrested,
every single night the Soviet Secret Police had knocked on Jadwiga's
door, pestering her about where I was hiding. She would wake up
at night in Sweden, screaming that someone was arresting her.
The horrors she lived through during her adolescence marked her
in unimaginable ways. She abhorred violence and oppression and
could not shake a lingering terror that it could all return.

Jadwiga's nightmares were not just about the terrible memories
of her last year in Poland. She also did not feel safe in Sweden.
Sweden had been a neutral country during World War II and had
allowed German troops to pass through Sweden to Finland. After
the war, the Swedes feared a Soviet invasion. Everyone I spoke
with was paranoid all the time about this because one day, a Soviet
cruiser came to Stockholm and demanded, from the Swedish

government, to hand over hundreds of Estonian political refugees. The Swedish newspapers reported the outrage that followed from their government handing over the refugees. My wife got scared that the next cruiser would come looking for Polish refugees. That's when we decided that we had to get to the U.S.

I applied for a visa to the U.S., but I was told that I would have to wait at least five years. Thankfully, it turned out that it would only be two years. When we received the good news about the visa, I decided to explore U.S. job opportunities and responded to a letter advertising work in New York. There were so many international words in the letter that were in commerce and trade language that I was able to understand it, despite not knowing English very well. I typed a response letter and gave it to my boss to sign, and he signed it without knowing what he was signing, due to it being in English. My boss was Bengt Laurén at Leed Shipping. He owned the third largest company in Sweden. They imported tractors and automobiles from England, France, and other countries. My wife always thought he was a very strange man, but I enjoyed working for him and appreciated him signing my letters of interest for jobs in the U.S.

At last, it was time to embark the MS Stockholm ship in Gothenburg, Sweden. Dr. Malmsten's wife Disa gave us a gift of two sets of silver tableware with knives, forks, and spoons. She told us, "You will need to have something to eat with when you arrive in the USA." We were very touched by this gesture, and showed the silverware to the Malmstens' daughter Birgitta when she and her brother Göran visited us over fifty years later in California.

Jadwiga Haska with Mrs. Disa Malmsten and Dr. Herbert Malmsten (front), the Swedish couple who assisted Jadwiga and Tadeusz when they were refugees. Lidköping, Sweden, 1948.

CHAPTER 5

Life in New York and California as a Polish Immigrant

When we immigrated to New York through Ellis Island on February 26, 1949, Jadwiga cried as she set her eyes on the beautiful Statue of Liberty. She said to me, "Now that I am fully free, I am not afraid anymore." She never had nightmares of being arrested again after that. Jadwiga also vowed never to go back to Poland, and she never did.

At Ellis Island, I did not realize how dangerous it was, because they could have separated us by sending me back to Sweden. After inspecting the x-rays of my lungs and my wife's lungs, they let my wife in right away but instructed me to wait. Many doctors were called over to look at my x-rays, and they were unsure at first, but eventually let me join my wife. I felt very relieved that I was not sent back.

When I was being questioned at Ellis Island, I was asked where I learned English. They thought I sounded like I was from Fair Isle in northern Scotland. I said something like, "That's okay with me, whatever you say." I was just happy to be there. My Swedish friends later told me that some of the people I was around in Sweden came from the mountains and spoke a distinct Swedish-English that sounds like the dialect spoken in Fair Isle, Scotland.

Once we were cleared at Ellis Island, my cousin Wanda Haska Bara and her husband Felix greeted us and invited us to their home. They let us stay in a two-room apartment or studio in their house on Long Island in a very nice area. We arrived on a Saturday. On Sunday, I bought the *New York Times* newspaper. When I put it on the floor in the living room and opened the pages, I found a job for my wife immediately: painter of ceramic china. On Monday, my cousin Wanda took us by subway to the Castleton China ceramic studio at 212 Fifth Avenue, where they made some of the finest china in the world. Jadwiga only had one small piece of paper, a certificate from the place she worked in Sweden called Rörstrand.

The director of Castleton China was a Danish fellow, Lundt, who personally knew the artist Carl-Harry Stålhane in Rörstrand who signed the certificate. When he saw the certificate, he immediately said, "You're hired!" There was a line of American job-seekers carrying pictures of the art they had been doing, and yet Jadwiga somehow got the job. But there was still one more hurdle for her to overcome before being hired.

She needed the approval of the French administrator of the company. When the administrator saw her, he looked at her skeptically and gave Jadwiga something to paint with a brush. As soon as he saw the way she took the brush in her fingers, he said, "You're hired." He did not even need to see her paint. He saw that she was a professional by the way that she held the brush. He became a very good friend to Jadwiga later on and paid her well for her work.

My cousin Wanda was somewhat bothered by Jadwiga working. She and her husband thought that they could get me a job working in some office, but they never thought that Jadwiga would be able to get a job. Wanda told us that, in the Haska family, men work, and women stay home, taking care of the family. This was considered a revolutionary situation that Jadwiga got a job while I was unemployed for a while. Wanda was upset by this, but my wife was happy.

Right to left—Jadwiga with Tad's cousins Ellie Haska, Wanda Haska Bara, and Wanda's husband Felix Bara. New York, about 1950.

Now that Jadwiga was working, I would leave the apartment at 2:00 a.m. each morning to get the *New York Times* newspaper to look for job advertisements for myself. I went early so that I could get it before anyone else. For the first job, I noticed that when I went to line up at the employer at 2:30 a.m., there was already a line extending three or four blocks long, full of American men wearing military decorations. It was 1949, and they had just returned from war. And I was a foreigner! I called myself a double foreigner because first I was a foreigner in Sweden, and now I was a foreigner in the U.S. I had no chance to get a job whatsoever because there were only three to five jobs available and three hundred men in line. I went to employer after employer, and it was the same story for several weeks.

After a month without a job, I went to an employment office organized by the Polish Catholic Church for Polish immigrants on Seventh Street in downtown New York. The priest tried to find Polish-American employers for immigrants. The head of the office was the former Minister of Labor in Poland who had escaped the German occupation. He told me, "I'm willing to give you any job opportunity I can find you, but your hands are not those of a manual laborer, so your chances of getting a job are slim right now."

But finally, one day, he told me, "Mr. Haska, I have something for you. It is a good job, relatively speaking, of course, but it is a good job." He gave me a letter of recommendation to give to a man named Mr. Malino. I thought he was Italian, but it turned out that he was a Polish man named Malinowski who pretended to be Italian. He was head of a department at Horn & Hardart that operated one hundred twenty-five restaurants in New York. One was called Automat for busy New Yorkers. There were vending machines where people would deposit some nickels into certain windows in a wall, and coffee, prepared sandwiches, and such would come out.

On Eleventh Avenue, Mr. Malino had a factory where they baked the bread served in the restaurants. About three hundred people were in front of me in line, applying for the job. But the man from the employment office told me not to wait in line but to ask for Mr. Malino directly because he knew I was coming. He was as huge as a football player for the New York Giants. When I introduced myself, Mr. Malino said, "Oh yes, you are expected. Just go get a certificate from the doctor to say that you are healthy since this is a food-producing place. Then come back."

Jadwiga did not want me to take this job baking bread, because she was making good money, and thought that I was overqualified for this job. She wanted me to continue my schooling. But I needed the job to prove to myself that I could work in the U.S. I wanted to bring home the bacon—not be a parasite. When I would later tell this story to people, Jadwiga would always say, "Tad always wanted to prove something to himself, like getting rid of the Communists. But look where that got him in Poland. In jail!"

When I returned to the restaurant with the document from my doctor, Mr. Malino took me to the bakery and told the foreman, "This is your new worker." I was left alone in a huge hall full of bread machines. Each worker was operating one machine for eight hours. I asked the workers why they did not periodically switch to a different machine, and they told me that when their muscles are accustomed to one particular machine, it frees their mind to think of other things while doing mechanical work. I soon realized that I was not made that way, so I jumped from one machine to another. When a worker needed a restroom or smoke break, I offered to take over their machine. So this way another set of muscles was getting exercised. When the worker returned, I jumped to another machine, and another set of muscles was getting exercised. This is how I was able to survive; otherwise, I would not have been able to do it.

I often worked a nightshift from about 11:00 p.m. to 4:00 a.m. New York was safe in 1949, even at night. I took the subway and walked for quite a while, and nobody would bother me—not at 11:00 p.m. or 4:00 a.m. While working at this job, I continued my schooling during the time that I was not at work.

While working at the bakery operating the different machines, I noticed that some workers had a different job from the rest. Four men were charged with unloading bread rolls and putting them in the oven. Nine loaves fit on a board, which had to be removed from underneath them, leaving them on the assembly line. The four workers had to be quick because the assembly line was moving, and the loaves had to be a certain distance from each other so that they did not squash each other. After the men removed the board, they would take another board with nine loaves and do the same thing. I noticed that these guys were doing this work for only four hours near the tremendous heat of the oven. The remaining four hours they would be downstairs in the delivery room, where they would load trucks with rolls and bread.

There was a nice cool temperature downstairs, so I viewed these four men as aristocrats and started dreaming, *How can I become one of those workers? What strategy should I use?* And I asked my foreman, "How about I work there?"

He said, "No such thing. These people have worked here for fourteen years, and they would never trade their jobs for yours. They are our aristocrats. This is a special job for them, and we cannot do anything about it. That's not for you, so forget about it."

But one day, one of these four men dropped dead at work. Very unfortunate for him, but very fortunate for me. My Swedish friend Birgitta, daughter of Dr. Malmsten who helped me survive in Sweden, says that there is an old Swedish saying that applies to this incident: "One's dead, the other's bread."

I was not standing far away from the poor man when he died, so I jumped right into his job, and not much time had passed, so not too much bread had accumulated. I proved that I could do that job.

The foreman came, and he was amazed. *"You* did this? Without training? How did you get this skill? Did you work in a mechanical bakery before?"

I answered, "Never in my life, but I just saw that this man fell, and they took him away, so I jumped right in his place because I thought it was the right thing to do."

The foreman later came back with the owner of the company, and they came to watch me do the job. They admired me, and I did not think it was anything to admire; I just jumped right into the job. I had thought it would be a shame to let the bread go to waste with the worker gone. The owner said, "You have a future here." Then the foreman started speaking to me as if I was a very important person.

After some time working there, I decided to leave for another job. The foreman started to pull his hair and said, "What are you doing leaving? You have a career here. You will not be here in this job long—you will be in our top office soon. We already discussed sending you there."

The reason I left that job is that the day before, I was leaving work and suddenly two men grabbed me and threw me into a car. I jumped through the other side of the car and somehow was able to get across four lanes of traffic of this busy street. I did not understand what had just happened. I quickly got to the subway station and disappeared.

Only later on, I started to think, *What could have caused that to happen?* Then I realized that it was because I made the same mistake

I made in Sweden. At work in the New York bakery restroom, workers had been asking me to tell my story and how I arrived there. I felt safe in the U.S., so I was stupid enough to tell them that I was a political refugee from Poland who had tried to fight the Communist system by running for office to help establish a democratic system.

A co-worker from Haiti was interested in my story. I did not speak very fluent English, but he spoke French, so I spoke with him in French. He asked, "Why did you oppose Communism—the system of justice for the people?" My wife always called it nonsense when someone would refer to Communism as justice.

Anyway, the Haitian became angry and said, "You are on the other side. What are you doing working here? You must be some kind of capitalist. Oh, and yesterday the owner of the shop came and talked to you! You are one of *them.*" The day after I told him my story, the two strangers tried to kidnap me. I think the Haitian had something to do with it because I never did anything wrong to anybody at that job.

Fortunately, I got another job fairly quickly. It was a position in a Polish-American fraternal organization that had an insurance company for Americans of Polish descent and published a newspaper. I was not very well paid, but it was still a nice position. My wife was enjoying a very good position with the china painting company.

One day I was in my boss's office when he was not in there and noticed that there was a letter addressed to the organization looking for instructors to teach Polish to American military personnel at the Army Language School in Monterey, California. I was surprised that my boss, the manager of the insurance office, did not tell me about the job announcement. I made a little note of who was sending the letter, put it in my pocket, and did not say anything. I expected that my boss would call me into his office and tell me about this job posting. Three days passed, and I decided that he probably was not planning to tell me because he wanted to keep me working for him. When he went to another room, I made a copy of the letter and sent a telegram to the Army Language School offering my services as a teacher of Polish. The next day I received a telegram asking me to come for an interview to Monterey. I was thrilled when they offered me the job.

When I told my boss that I would be leaving, he became angry and said, "Why would you want to live there? New York is America. California is where wild Indian savages live, jumping from tree to tree. You are going there to this wilderness? Forget about it. I have a request on my desk for teachers of Polish but never thought you'd want to go there. America is New York, and New York is America. There is no future in California." I don't think that he knew for sure that I had seen the job notice on his desk.

Meanwhile, my wife Jadwiga had been enjoying her job painting china. Rich customers asked her to paint specific items in a certain way. Sometimes she did not agree with the color or style they selected, but she always followed their instructions. When she was pregnant with our daughter Christine and still working, she did not want her boss to know until as late in the pregnancy as possible. She told her friend and co-worker at the studio not to mention to their boss that she was pregnant.

However, at the office Christmas party in 1950, each person was expected to exchange a small gift with someone else in the studio. When Jadwiga opened her gift from her co-worker, she was surprised to see that it was baby clothes. When the president of the company insisted on seeing her gift, he demanded to know who would inappropriately give this gift to someone who was not pregnant (because Jadwiga was not showing yet). Jadwiga stood up so that he could see that she was pregnant. She did not want her co-worker to be reprimanded, so she admitted that she was expecting. Her boss was very kind and indicated that he would pay for her maternity leave, insurance, and for someone else to take care of the baby if she wanted to work part-time after the baby's arrival. She was treated very well in return for being a good employee. The china she was painting cost one to four thousand dollars for a set of twelve, which was a lot of money at the time. Jadwiga eventually told her boss that she would be moving to California, and he promised to make sure that all of her maternity needs were taken care of before her departure. The ladies in her studio surprised her with countless baby dresses to celebrate our daughter's birth.

It was an exciting time because our daughter Christine was born by emergency C-section on April 25, 1951. We called her Christine (Krysia in Polish) because of a dream Jadwiga experienced while in labor.

I felt bad leaving my wife and baby so soon, but I kept getting messages from the Army Language School saying that I had better report to the job now or it would be given to somebody else. I had already postponed the trip until after the baby was born, and I could not postpone it any longer. Jadwiga said, "It is a good job for us, so you have to go." It would be several months before she and the baby were able to join me.

Jadwiga Haska with daughter Christine in Jackson Heights, New York, 1951.

So, the day after our daughter's birth, I boarded a train to California on April 26. My cousins were opposed to me flying due to air accidents we had heard about. They said, "You'll be dead on the way to California. It is much safer by rail." It took me three and a half days to get to California, but I saw a lot of the U.S. from the train, and it was a very nice trip.

I started the job at the end of April 1951. Eisenhower was not president yet, but he was campaigning, and he was proclaiming a crusade against Communism. All the minorities in the U.S. like the Polish, Czechs, and Hungarians, who were subjugated by

Communism, wanted freedom. So, the Army Language School was recruiting instructors for all those eastern European languages, and those departments were growing tremendously. Russian was the largest department, but Polish was also becoming very large. When Eisenhower became president, he somehow forgot about this crusade he had used as part of his campaign message.

In any case, I was teaching Polish to English-speaking American members of the armed forces. It was not as easy as it would seem. It was all about drilling, like constantly crushing stones on the road. I had to correct my students' pronunciation, repeat things hundreds of times, and show how to form their lips and tongue to achieve a particular sound. I required them to look into a mirror while they were saying the words to observe their lip movements. It required a lot of patience. I am not saying that I did not feel fit for the job. Quite the contrary, the greater the difficulties, the better I managed. I never showed up unprepared. Having everything ready meant there were no surprises. I taught by total immersion, speaking Polish only. This method proved to be very successful because within almost twelve months, students were able to understand, speak, read, and write Polish.

At first, we had a number of students of Polish descent who spoke some Polish at home and then were sent to Monterey to get a refresher course according to army requirements. But later on, students who never had any Polish, and even some who had never heard of Poland, were sent there. We were successful with them too.

We were actually more successful with them than with those who knew some Polish—those students sometimes opposed our efforts to teach them "our" Polish instead of their "kitchen Polish" they learned from their parents spoken fifty years ago. They were very reluctant to learn our kind of Polish. They said, "Mother and Father taught us this way, and now you're teaching us another way? No, I don't like it." And we had to fight it. So, it was easier to teach someone who did not know anything about Polish than someone who knew some Polish. Also, the ones who knew some Polish were often speaking different dialects from various regions of Poland. As instructors, we were not supposed to teach dialects. We were supposed to teach the official radio/newspaper/literary dialect of Polish common to all Poles, whether they were from the east, west, north, or south.

I found that my experience in Sweden listening to the Linguaphone records helped me be a better teacher. At the Army Language School, students would sometimes complain about not getting anything out of the Polish tapes they were instructed to listen to. I shared with them my experience of learning English and encouraged them to keep tally marks of the number of times they listened to each tape in order to check their progress. The more they did this, the more successful they were as students. Of course, Jadwiga later said the students' wives told her that this method drove their wives crazy.

Every day I attended other instructors' lectures to learn about their methods. Everyone was polite and friendly. We also were expected to experience learning a new language so that we could sympathize with our students. During the Danish lesson, I made quite an impression on everyone because I knew everything. Of course, I did not say a word to give away that I spoke Swedish. Everyone was amazed, and the Danish teacher kept shaking his head. My colleagues started to see me as a linguist. This was especially gratifying for me because I was the youngest among the instructors, and felt I had to prove myself to my colleagues. The head of the Polish department, Mr. Stefan Kaminski, gave me special jobs to do that other instructors were not given. I liked him very much.

Tadeusz Haska working as an instructor at the Army Language School in 1951.

I enjoyed my job but missed my family. Back in New York, there was a christening party for my daughter without me. I lived in barracks bachelor quarters while I waited for them to join me. It was a very pleasant type of a job, and I was finally doing what I was trained for. But the time apart from my wife and newborn baby was very hard on us.

Jadwiga worried that we would not have enough money in California and tried to persuade me to return to New York. I told her that we were young and could earn enough money. I reminded her that we lost everything at one time and managed to get back on our feet. I also reminded her that California would be a safer place to raise our family. We could sleep peacefully there, even if a war broke out. I told Jadwiga that it would be more likely for a raid to occur in New York than in California, and Stalin would not say a word beforehand. Another way I tried to persuade her that moving here was the right decision was by talking about the air quality, wide open green areas, and lack of New York heat waves. I even told her that people lived longer in Monterey. In an area with forty-five thousand people, there was only one funeral service company, so I reasoned that not many people died in Monterey!

Presidio of Monterey 8 June 1951

My dearest darling:

How is our Krysia? How are you feeling? Monterey is a health resort. You have not seen such a beautiful place in your entire life. You are my sweet little green frog. All alone and forlorn. When will I have you here and when will we enjoy our life together? I am going to send you 60 dollars from my next wages—just like you said, or if you want, 80. Today is Friday evening. Two days of weekend without you. My God, I feel so sad here without you, my lovely darlings. Your life is always so hard, my darling. Your fate is always so bad for you. Even now—you don't have your parents near you, and I am so far away. But let's hope you'll be able to come here soon. What do you think? It will be good for both you and Krysia. You'll be able to breathe the fresh air as much as you want. You, of course, will moan and worry about this or that just as you like, and I will cheer you up and convince you that life is beautiful, and the world is also beautiful. You like this, so you'll be happy, and together we will be happy. You are my clever lady who always thinks ahead and who always likes to know what to look forward to.

Bye, my love—kisses for our little Krysia
from her daddy Tad.

Jadwiga gave me quite a hard time in her letters to me, frequently explaining how I should move back to New York with her. In my last letter to her from Monterey, I could finally report that I had secured a new apartment for us and made the arrangements for her long-awaited arrival.

Ord Village 7 July 1951

My dearest wife,

And so I am now at our new apartment. Our apartment is beautiful: 2 bedrooms, living room, kitchen, bathroom. There are a few trees. I can already see you are going to enjoy your life here, my sweet little darling. Our Krysia and you will feel very comfortable here. Here you will enjoy the life you have always dreamed of. There is just one thing. You will need to get used to a siren which sounds at 12:00 and 5:00. That's the only minus. You are not allowed to take a plane. Firstly, it is dangerous. Secondly, you will not get 150 pounds of free baggage to transport all the stuff, you would need to pay for every pound. With the train, you will only need to pay for what's over the 150 pounds. You need to book the tickets immediately. The train is called a "Zephyr." Here when one lady joined her husband, she was told that if she wanted to take the Zephyr, she would have needed to book the tickets three weeks in advance. Zephyr is known to be the best train. If you take the roomette, you wouldn't need to change in Chicago, but you would travel straight to San Francisco. Make sure you reach S.F. on Saturday so I can collect you. How is the apartment sale going? What do you think?

When will you be able to get here? Write to me how things are.

From my side, I sorted everything; the house is top-notch, and I am just waiting for my lovely family. It has been a torture without my darlings and then it has been a torture for you without me. But now things are about to change. Do you love me? You'll be able to dry your linen in the fresh air. I'm not sure about a washing machine, though. If there is any available... You made your statement to me quite clearly that we need to be reunited by the end of this month and I played a little trick on you because you can arrive practically any time now. Look how quickly I got this sorted out. In every letter, you were giving me your lessons on how I need to sort out the house as soon as possible. You told me off a few times, and now you can see that your husband is able to sort something out. Tell me so... Anyway, lots of kisses for you and our Krysia and write to me how you both are. You should book the ticket now.

Your loving husband and father of Krysia,

Tad

After three months, her doctor permitted Jadwiga to travel, and, at last, my wife and daughter joined me in California. At first, we lived in the military barracks at Ord Village, which were for military personnel's families. Later on, we rented an apartment in Monterey on Franklin Street. In a few months, we bought a house on 56 Cuesta Vista Drive. We were very happy. We had a child, house, and security. We felt that we could live now like normal people, not refugees anymore.

Tadeusz Haska with daughter Christine in Monterey, California
in the early 1950s.

When Christine was growing up, we only spoke Polish to her. Even though she was born in the U.S., English was her second language. She did not speak any English until she went to school. I felt that she should be able to communicate with her parents in their language. I explained to her kindergarten teacher that I wanted her to learn correct English without our accent. Christine's Polish is just like our Polish, and she always excelled in English. So I believe in the principle that languages should develop independently of each other. She spoke Polish at home and English everywhere else. Language centers are in a particular area of the brain. If languages are intertwined (such as during translation), then those languages don't develop independently, and mastery cannot be achieved. My theory proved correct in my daughter's case.

Tadeusz Haska with daughter
Christine wearing Polish folk
costume in Monterey, California
at Language Day at the Defense
Language Institute in the late 1950s.

After a number of years, I went to UC-Berkeley for six months to finish my U.S. bachelor's degree in Slavic Languages and Literature in 1962. There was a residency requirement, so I had to live in Berkeley during that time. They recognized the courses that I took at university in Poland. One kind professor objected to the evaluation of my credits from Poland because he felt that I was not given enough credits and believed that I should have been given the bachelor's degree without having to attend Berkeley for six months. After the bachelor's degree, I was admitted straight to the Ph.D. program at Berkeley (without having to get a master's degree first), but I would have had to resign from my job, so I decided to get my master's degree in history by commuting to San Jose State University, taking courses in European history.

I commuted two to three times a week, sometimes in the evening, and earned my master's degree in 1967. Salaries for instructors teaching Slavic languages weren't high at the time. My friend, who was a full professor with three hundred publications in the Slavic department, showed me his pay stub at the university, and he only made $12,000 per year in 1961. But he was proud of how much he made. Yet I was making $10,000 at the Army School, and I did not want to lose that good job. So, I did not resign from my job.

Keeping my full-time job at the Army School, I went back to Berkeley with a scholarship to study for my Ph.D., which I earned in

1976. The master's degree I earned was not necessary to get my Ph.D., but it allowed me to get my Ph.D. with one less year of study. Jadwiga helped support our family by working as a maid in a hotel, and later as a nurse. In 1972, I was thrilled to be promoted to chairman of the Polish Department.

Tadeusz Haska teaching Polish at the Army Language School in Monterey.

Eventually, the Army Language School changed its name to the Defense Language Institute, and it expanded to serve all branches of the military and even the FBI. The program was not just for teaching languages, but for developing curricula, and writing textbooks. Some branches of the military wanted specialized courses. For instance, some were interested in speaking a language, but others wanted comprehension or writing or reading, and some wanted all four skills.

The school is still in operation today. Some departments have been increasing while others are decreasing. Polish was constantly growing when I was there. We had twenty-six instructors during the Eisenhower crusade (when he was campaigning against Communism) but dropped to twelve when he was president. When the solidarity movement appeared in Poland in the 1970s, the department grew again; at the time of the silent revolution, it grew to fifty instructors. Now there is no Polish department; what remains is a branch of a multi-language department where other small units remain such as Czech, and German. Now the Arabic, Russian, Chinese, and Spanish departments are large.

After five years in the U.S., we became citizens at a ceremony in San Francisco. There was an examination of our potential as citizens. We passed and were very happy finally to be normal people. We were not refugees anymore. We were American citizens! To celebrate, we took a family trip to Disneyland in 1956, a year after its opening. Jadwiga's mother joined us. After Jadwiga's father, Jan Trzebiński, died in Poland in 1953, we were blessed to have her mother, Władysława Trzebińska, come to live with us in 1956 until her death in 1980. My brother Antoni and his wife Maria visited us in Monterey in 1981. They did not often visit because they did not speak English, but I visited Antoni periodically in Poland in the 1990s and 2000s. He graduated from the Academy of Fine Arts in Kraków after the war and became a well-known artist and teacher.

Building painted by Antoni Haska in Poznań, Poland after his graduation from the Academy of Fine Arts in Kraków.

I enjoyed working at the Defense Language Institute for thirty-five years before retiring in 1986. Although I was not able to stay in Poland to fulfill my dream of helping to make it a democracy, I believe I was able to make more of an impact by teaching students in the West who would take the skills I taught them to the East. My knowledge of languages helped keep me alive during and after the war, and I was fortunate to make a career out of my passion for linguistics. To be happy, it is important to find work you love and someone to share your life with.

Tadeusz Haska receiving an award at the Defense Language Institute in Monterey, California. Jadwiga and Tadeusz Haska at home in Monterey, California in June 1968. Artwork in the background is by Tadeusz's brother Antoni.

I could not have made it here without my loving Jadwiga, who passed away on October 19, 2003. She defined strength for me from my earliest memories with her to our last days together. She loved me and trusted me to smuggle her out of Poland when her family thought I was crazy. I always felt bad that my Jadwiga had to face the war as an innocent teenager, seeing unspeakable horror, and then face the death of our son alone, when we were waiting to be reunited. Yet she came out of it all with hope and determination. Her dream was a world without war and freedom for everyone. She always said, "Count your blessings. Don't complain; you could have real problems. Look at all the people who are sick and alone in the world!" This would be her response to any complaint or whining about something.

Although Jadwiga was too afraid to ever return to Poland, we went to Rome to celebrate our fiftieth wedding anniversary in September 1996, and enjoyed a private audience with Saint John Paul II, along with our daughter, granddaughter, and grandson-in-law.

Tadeusz and Jadwiga celebrating their 50th wedding anniversary in Rome after a private audience with Saint John Paul II.

Jadwiga's devotion to family and the nobility of serving others always came first. Her life was focused on making a nice home for us. She lived her faith and love. She set a new standard for grandmothering. When our granddaughter Stefanie was born, there was a light that shined in her. She adored that baby in a way that everyone who knew her could see. For every stage of Stefanie's life, Jadwiga was an enthusiastic presence—urging her on, bursting with pride.

The last two years of Jadwiga's life, as she faced Alzheimer's disease, were devastating for her and all of our family. But even through the most difficult moments, I saw glimmers of her will—her determination. When she could not find the right words to connect with what she wanted to communicate, her eyes would fire with frustration. When she needed assistance with moving, she would at times wave us away so that she could do things her own way. She accepted our love, but she wanted to assert herself in our world until the end. I admire her, and I feel blessed to have been her husband.

Jadwiga's death was a blow, and I'm still trying to recover from it. I am comforted by the love of my daughter Christine, granddaughter Stefanie, grandson-in-law David, and great-grandchildren Emily and Alex.

In March 2000, our daughter Christine was invited to go to Parliament in Poland, while visiting a university in Poland through her job at Rutgers University. At Parliament, she told them that her father tried to be a member of Parliament in 1947, but she was now speaking on his behalf. She enjoyed the honor of meeting Solidarity movement leader and President of Poland (1990–1995) Lech Wałęsa. Having her speak for me at the Polish Parliament was a wonderful way for my life story to come full circle.

Tadeusz Haska's daughter, Christine, with Lech Wałęsa at Polish Parliament in March 2000.

Family Photos

Brothers Tadeusz and Antoni Haska.

Tadeusz and Jadwiga Haska in Monterey, California.

Alex Naumann, Tadeusz Haska, Stefanie Naumann,
Emily Naumann, David Naumann.

Family Christmas Celebrations

Jadwiga and Tadeusz Haska.

Polish tradition of exchanging the opłatek wafer at Christmas.

David Naumann, Stefanie Naumann, Christine Haska,
Tadeusz Haska, Jadwiga Haska.

Tadeusz Haska's 90th Birthday at Kona Village, Hawaii, 2009

Tadeusz Haska with great-grandchildren Alex and Emily Naumann.

Tadeusz Haska
and his grandaughter
Stefanie Brown Naumann

Gdansk

BIBLIOGRAPHY

Haska, Tadeusz Leon. Personal documents, journals, photo albums, and interviews captured via audio and video recordings in 1989, 1990, 2005, 2006, and 2009.

Amelia Łaczyńska i jej wspomnienia. Wybór i opracowanie J. Sroka (w:) *Darłowskie Zeszyty Muzealne* , Nr 1, *Darłowo, Zamek Książąt Pomorskich*, 2017, s.17-43 The Library in Kórnik, Poland contains the orginal diaries of Amelia *Łaczyńska*. The passages that mention Tadeusz Haska appear on pages 24, 30-31.

Aleksander Tarnowski , 12 lat na Zamku w Darłowie (w:) Zaraz po wojnie. Zapis pierwszego dwudziestolecia we wspomnieniach osadników w powiecie sławieńskim, red. J. Sroki, Sławno 2009, s. 97-226. The passages that mention Tadeusz Haska appear on page 145.

Sroka, Jan. *Znani Nieznani Mieszkańcy Powiatu Sławieńskiego (Famous and unknown inhabitants of the Sławski county).* Sławno: Fundacja "Dziedzictwo," 2018.

Walkiewicz, Leszek, and Żukowski, Marek. *Darłowo, Zarys dziejów. Darłowo, 2005. (Darłowo, Outline of History, Part III, p. 227).*

Stefanie Naumann may be contacted

at Stefanie@StefanieNaumann.com

Lightning Source UK Ltd.
Milton Keynes UK
UKHW041434280520
363988UK00005B/1536